SWEAT OF THE SUN TEARS OF THE MOON

Wild and delightful... The sense of emancipation experienced by the wanderer from the Old World is indescribably sweet and novel... How refreshing to meet with perfect freedom of intercourse tempered only by the innate courtesy and native grace of the Spanish Americans... May the blight of our superior civilization never fall on (them).

W H Hudson *The Purple Land* 1885

SWEAT OF THE SUN TEARS OF THE MOON

IN SOUTH AMERICA WITH JACK PIZZEY

Macdonald
Queen Anne Press

A Queen Anne Press BOOK

© Australian Broadcasting Corporation 1985, 1986

First published in Australia in 1985 by ABC Enterprises for the
Australian Broadcasting Corporation, Sydney
First published in Great Britain in 1986 by
Queen Anne Press, a division of
Macdonald & Co (Publishers) Ltd
Greater London House, Hampstead Road
London NW1 7QX

A BPCC plc Company

British Library Cataloguing in Publication Data
Pizzey, Jack
   Sweat of the sun, tears of the moon.
   1. South America — Description and travel
   — 1981 -
   I. Title
   918'.0438   F2225

   ISBN 0-356-12697-8

Printed and bound in Great Britain by
Hazell Watson & Viney Limited
Member of the BPCC Group
Aylesbury, Bucks

CONTENTS

INCA COLA

CHAPTER 1

In the year that was to come we would travel South America from frozen peak to palm tree coast, from lush jungle to seared desert. We would film in palaces and in slums. We would samba in the Rio *Carnaval,* ride the Pampas with Argentine *gauchos,* perch precariously in Amazon canoes. We would eat monkey with missionaries, chew armadillo with *campesinos.* It would be the adventure of a lifetime, and probably the longest spell on location ever undertaken by a documentary team. But in my memory the story would always begin – perhaps because it almost ended then too – on a particular day in Bolivia. ¶That day began badly in small ways and grew worse. At dawn there were minor irritations, by evening it would be a question of whether we'd be allowed to live. To begin with, the thin air of the Andes had made it hard to sleep. Dry as a bone, sharp as a needle, the mountain air left our nostrils caked and our heads aching for oxygen. For the Indians it was no problem. They'd evolved barrel chests and big lungs, these descendants of the Inca empire, they were at home. But we were wheezing *gringos,* out of our element. And getting up before dawn in our tourists' hotel, we were lost even in our own rooms because the electricity was off. Bumping my way to the bathroom, I found the water off too. Using the cap of my aerosol foam shave I scooped water from the lavatory cistern and found my face with the razor.

Page Seven

Outside, down by the water, Indians were already moving in their un-hurried way among their fishing boats. The *Mickey Mouse* and the *Carmen* waited serenely to go out onto a Lake Titicaca paling from black to grey in the early light. It was going to be a fine Andean day. But, for us, the irritations continued: waiting by the ferry our driver told us *'Todavia hay huelga'* — the strike was still on. The ferry would take us across the lake, but the road from there to La Paz was blocked at one of the villages. The Indians over there were still protesting. In the usual way, the driver said, 'rocks across the road'. Already this had delayed us twenty-four hours and now we were full of *gringo* impatience: we had a filming schedule to keep to. Pablo the driver was impatient too. He'd made all the prepara-tions, roped a large drum of petrol to the roof of his old creamy Chevvy, and we weren't getting anywhere. 'We could', he suggested, 'try driving up to that village and offering them some money to let us pass their road block'.

Driving up from the far shore of the lake, with the ferry left behind us, we screwed up our eyes looking for the first sign of the road block. By now the morning was bright, and the lake below was as royal a blue as water can ever be. The road block, when it came in sight, seemed to be peacefully in harmony with the Andean day — scattered rocks on the road to halt our approach, then a tree trunk across the asphalt and a few dozen Indians standing around in the warm Bolivian sun. Pablo stopped the car about forty paces short of the tree trunk, got out, walked forward. I sat in the back and waited. Next to me was my wife, Gloria, next to her was the Producer, Geoff. Gloria was from Colombia, a descendant of the Spanish invaders who had crushed the Incas four centuries before and who had kept the Indians in subjection ever since. Geoff was Australian. We were white and, even forty paces away from the brown Indians who now commanded the road, we felt conspicuous.

When Pablo had got out of the car to go and negotiate no word had been needed — we had known we should stay inside. Pablo was brown, part Indian. His Inca blood was the same as theirs. We were outsiders, the colour of the old conquerors and still the colour — on any day but this, in any place but this — of power and authority.

We saw Pablo speak with a group of Indians, we saw him turn and come back towards us. Behind him they began to move rocks from our path and to drag the tree trunk to one side. Pablo reached us again, started the Chevvy and drove up past the Indians. As we squeezed through, one of them patted the roof approvingly and we settled back for the two-hour drive across the *Altiplano* to La Paz. The high plain opened out on either side, a flat valley with an icy gravel floor, edged with crumpled grey hills and white peaks. We would be in La Paz in time for lunch. But a few minutes later, rounding a curve, we saw ahead of us the mud-walled houses of another village, with the rocks and the standing figures of another road block. Again Pablo stopped the car well short of them and walked forward. Again money changed hands, rocks were moved, the Chevvy eased forward. Gaining speed to make up for lost time now Pablo explained the reason for the second road block: the people had heard about the first one and decided to have a protest of

(Page 6) 'Compreme!' *— Buy from me! Souvenir seller at Lake Titicaca.*

their own. At the first village the protest had been over some land requisitioned by the government, at the second it had been over low prices for the local maize.

At the next village it was meat prices, at the next taxes. Every village on the *Altiplano* was venting its grievances in rocks and tree trunks. As we learned later, this road block rebellion often happens at times of unrest in Bolivia, and, it's best not to be on the roads if your skin is white. Not that there was any danger during the first part of the afternoon — just the irritation of repeated delays, and the expense of a handful of *pesos* for Pablo to give to each new band of roadside rebels. But at the road blocks of the late afternoon the mood was changing. At every stop we'd seen Indians drinking. Always there were pots of *chicha*. And now the maize beer was having its effect. Whereas the faces of the morning had been relaxed if never actually friendly, those of the late afternoon were frightening. Now no Indian patted the Chevvy's roof as we eased through the barricades, now they looked coldly through us. Knitted helmets framed their wide cheekbones, and to meet their eyes was to meet what? Nothing at all? An indifference implying that you didn't exist? They seemed to look right past us at some vista of four hundred and fifty years of domination by men with skins like ours.

Now each road block became a threat, and each new crowd of Indians on the road ahead caused a flutter in the stomach. Pablo was having difficulty deciding who to pay, no one was in charge any more. If one broad hand came forward to take the *pesos,* so would another, and another. Then Pablo would drive us slowly into the crowd chatting through the window to ease his *gringo* passengers past the reaching hands and the faces that began to come closer to the windows. We sat there — nervous, trying to look relaxed, increasingly afraid. In the atmosphere around us now even a small boy with a catapult suddenly became a possible executioner; the women in the shawls and bowler hats spinning yarn at the roadside could become the ladies of the guillotine; youths with jugs of beer in one hand and flaming torches in the other eyed the drum of petrol on our roof.

That brought to my mind the words of one of the Spaniards who had been with Pizarro's tiny force surrounded by Incas in 1532 — he wrote that some of his comrades were soiling themselves in their fear.

At one of the earlier road blocks a school teacher had asked us for a lift. She was a pretty light brown girl — a *mestiza.* But now when she saw how hot things were she left us suddenly and dived into the Indian crowd. It was dangerous to be in our company. That Pablo still stuck by us was remarkable. His car had been stopped. Now they were pressing all around it. Every window was packed with faces. They were pushing us slowly off the road. This road block we would not pass. And what was going to happen to us next seemed obvious.

One of the Indians — the boy with the catapult, the youth with the flaming torch — would make the first move. He would smash in a window or start to roll the car over, and we would become scapegoats for the wrongs of the *conquistadores.* I would have to watch my wife being raped, we would be robbed and burned and, in lawless Bolivia, forgotten.

(Left) No problems for her. Her Aymara skin was a passport through Indian road blocks.

(Below) 'The Indian is deliberate in all he does, generous with all he has, and hates to serve.'
(16th century Spanish Conquistador)

(Right) Country boy, Bolivia.

The car was tilted, sliding down the embankment towards the plain below, when the crowd's attention was caught by a new attraction: up on the road above us a bus was arriving at the road block and being forced to a halt. Drawn by this bigger prize, the crowd surged up the bank and left us. The last flaming torch disappeared above and we were alone. Switching off the headlamps Pablo began to steer along a path parallel to the road, a path that would take us unseen past the last of the road blocks and back to the capital. It had been a strong introduction to the people we'd come to learn about — the Andes Indians, the descendants of the Inca Impire.

In fact there probably never was a people called the Incas. There was a group who spoke *Quechua* and who were and still are sometimes called the 'Quechua', and their word for 'leader' was *inca*. Eventually that was how their whole civilisation came to be known, especially by the white invaders who destroyed it.

But though the empire is gone now, the idea of Inca identity is still alive. It is even perhaps growing stronger. At the old Inca town of Raqchi in Peru we saw this in a festival of Indian music. People came from all over the Peruvian Andes to dance and drink *chicha,* and to listen. Beneath Inca ruins like brown broken teeth, the women sang in tiny high voices, the dancers stamped and swayed in the stolid way of mountain people, and the rainbow flag of the Incas swelled and filled under the sun. That Inca flag has been invented only in recent years as a yearning has grown for some revival of the greatness of the most famous of the early South Americans. Evidently it makes an Indian feel good to think of himself as an Inca, and it impresses the whites too. 'We all admire the old Inca culture' you'll hear whites admit, 'It's just that we can't stand the Indians!' It seems that if you call a man an Indian you're putting him down, but call him an Inca and you put him up. The name 'Inca' even has commercial value — the brand name of Peru's most popular soft drink is, improbably, 'Inca Kola'.

So who were the Incas? What has been happening to them? And who are they now?

It is said that our history of the Incas is sixty per cent speculation, thirty per cent probability and only ten per cent established fact. So who they were is not easy to discover.

They had no writing, so their history lives only in what was written about them by their Spanish conquerors and in what they made and built.

What they built was impressive: massive agricultural terraces, great palaces and temples of interlocking carved boulders, roads from one end of the craggy empire to the other, and one city which is a wonder of the world. None of all the films and photos and picture post cards of it can prepare you for the experience of actually seeing Machu Picchu, the lost city of the Incas miraculously perched on the peaks as sheer as jungle-clad steeples.

But I think that what Machu Picchu really tells us about the Incas is not that they were great architects — after all, long before the Incas built Machu Picchu the Greeks had built the Parthenon, a building

(Above) Inca fortress above terraces that once fed thousands. Pisac, Peru.

(Right) Machu Picchu.

which aesthetically eclipses the Inca design. What Machu Picchu tells us is that the Incas were great organisers. To have imagined building on such a peak, to have actually made it happen — that's where the Inca genius lay. It was that flair for organising that enabled them to take the remains of many earlier Indian civilisations and weld them into what was probably one of the most authoritarian states that man has yet devised.

At the head was The Inca, claimed to be the son of the sun — a relationship which gave him absolute power because the Inca people believed their race to be the children of the sun and the moon. So to challenge The Inca was to challenge God. And below was a rigid hierarchy that reached down, level by level, to the lowest Indian in the furthest corner of the empire of upwards of six million people with a hundred different ethnic groups speaking twenty languages, in a territory as big as the Roman Empire.

(Facing page) The Inca
Lives! Festival of the Sun.
Cuzco, Peru.

(Above) King Atahuallpa
would turn in his grave!

(Left) Raqchi, Peru. They
dance for the sake of
dancing — not for tourists.
Yet.

You can see signs of the Inca hierarchy in the houses at Machu Picchu. There's one design for the priests, a lesser one for the soldiers, a still lesser one for the craftsmen. If you stand on the walls of Machu Picchu and look out, you can imagine that the empire still exists and that the ordered life of the fourteenth and fifteenth centuries is still proceeding in the valleys below. But down on the Peruvian coast there's another great relic of Indian times, and there such imaginings are soon dispelled. Pachacamac was once the largest city on the Pacific coast of the Americas. By the time the Incas acquired it, Indian civilisations had been blooming and withering for thousands of years in a South America not known, not even guessed at by anyone in Europe. But then came the Spanish. They stormed up the steep sandy slopes of Pachacamac, burst into its temple, seized the high priest and tortured him for gold, and made this city on the Pacific shore a part of their own empire. And now if you stand on top of Pachacamac among the ruins and drifting sand, you cannot dream, as you can at Machu Picchu, that the Incas still rule, because the proof that they don't is in view. Across the dunes is depressing evidence of what many of the Incas' descendants have become — outsiders, living in poverty. The evidence is a new slum, what in this part of South America they euphemistically call a *pueblo joven*, meaning a 'young town'. Young it is. Less than a year ago a few thousand Indians did what many others have done in the last twenty years. Faced with joblessness, homelessness, hopelessness, they formed themselves into a small force armed with sheets of cardboard and wattle. Then, under cover of night, they moved onto some barren land and put up homes. Beside every shack they planted a Peruvian flag, then they waited to see if the police would come and drive them away.

Now if you walk down the crumbled glory of Pachacamac to their 'town', they greet you with polite formality and an innocent pride in their achievement. 'Welcome to San Juan de Miraflores, *señor*, would you care to see our town?'

What they show you is reminiscent of refugee camps in the Middle East. Frail shacks in the sand, skinny children and dogs, women carrying leaky cans of water from the stand pipe, people with blank faces shuffling aimlessly past, an air of everlasting temporariness. The Indians here have become part of the great paradox of South America — that it is a rich land full of poor people.

How have the mighty Incas come to this? In the Inca empire famine was unknown and they would have been guaranteed food and a roof. But ever since the Spanish put their mark on South America, and right up until today, there has been no such security. Peru, the old heart of the Incas' world, today has acres of these cardboard towns, hectares of unrelieved Indian poverty.

That Inca Peru was able to feed and house everyone whereas modern Peru cannot seemed to us a paradox worth putting to the president. At the end of a bare stretch of sand edged by a few shacks which the elders of the shanty town optimistically told us would one day be 'The Avenue', we thanked them and headed back across the dunes towards the capital.

The road to Lima lay through colourless hills and slums, and under an almost perennial mist the city itself seemed a place where whatever was not grey was brown. Before our scheduled interview with the president there was time for lunch and a change into a suit at Lima's Gran Hotel Bolivar. From the greyness of the city founded four centuries ago by Pizarro, the Spanish conqueror, we stepped into the opulence of a hotel named for Simon Bolivar who had thrown off the Spanish yoke three centuries later.

Soft carpets, marbled corridors, an air of costly tranquillity. It could have been Paris, but in the Gran Bolivar's elegant terrace restaurant came a reminder that this was South America. Sitting at a neighbouring table was a crippled beggar. His ragged elbows rested confidently on the thick white table cloth, his withered legs dangled from the upholstered chair. It was clear that he had been invited up by the tourist who now sat facing him across cut glass and silver dishes. And host and guest were obviously enjoying their outrageous piece of anarchy. The effect on the waiters was what I wanted to watch. How would they treat the young upstart suddenly promoted from literally beneath their feet? Like many waiters in the more traditional hotels of South America they were oldish men who took a gentle pride in their work. Hovering around you in white gloves, they were warm and helpful like old family retainers in some long ago great house. Never intrusive, they were quietly delighted if they saw that you enjoyed the food. Their smiles above their starched white

(Above) one of the President's problems — the unemployed.

(Overleaf) Where Condors Fly. The Andes, three miles above sea level. Peru.

jackets were gentle, childlike. And now these brown men who'd worked their way up to a position in the smartest hotel in Pizarro's City of the Kings were faced with a young cripple from the gutter with his elbows on their sumptuous table linen.

I felt apprehensive, both for them and for the unlikely guest. Could their kindness possibly extend to cover him? Or would it now be revealed as a professional facade reserved for more conventional customers. Rather than concentrate on the questions I would be putting to the president later, I was watching for the first sign of some waiter's head held aloof, for the disdain, the snub that I felt must come. In London, in New York, in Paris, in Sydney, in a hundred restaurants I could think of, the snub would have been almost inevitable. But one of the attractions of the South Americans for me is their kindness. Despite all the poverty, the inequality, the injustice, you will find in the people a kindness and a gaiety almost unknown in our developed world. It is as though we have developed economically while the South Americans have developed emotionally. There was no snub, no curled lip. I realised that the waiters were actually enjoying themselves. Their smiles and their tender support for their special guest were spontaneous. These men were not put out, and they never for a moment patronised him. Perhaps they even felt a certain solidarity with him. At the end of the meal, they stood respectfully as he eased himself down from the chair and with his straight little legs trailing, slid on his hands and buttocks away along the marble floors of the Gran Bolivar and back to his place by the gutter outside.

Walking afterwards from the hotel to the presidential palace it seemed hard to believe that we were in the capital of a country that had once been the centre of an Indian empire. In flesh and blood there was plenty of evidence of Indians, stocky figures carrying bundles inside cloaks of red and brown. And their wide oriental faces were mirrored a thousand times in the people of mixed blood all around us who are now most of the population. But in the stone and masonry of the capital there was no trace of the Incas, no echo of their massive stone blocks and trapezoidal doorways. Looking up at Spanish balconies and porticos, at the uncompromisingly European bulk of the old cathedral, it wasn't hard to understand why. When the Spaniards had conquered the Incas they'd needed to impose their own ways; gothic arches and curlecued spires were part of their apparatus of dominance. That explained the absence of Indian character in the old buildings. But even in the more recent ones, built long after any need to suppress the Indians must have faded, there was no sign of any acknowledgment of Peru's great Inca past.

The presidential palace, when we reached it, was a fine example of architecture ignoring the Incas. Though it had been rebuilt only thirty-five years ago, it was entirely a thing of Europe. In front of a baroque facade the scarlet and white palace guards jerked in a ponderous goose-step to trumpets blaring the Grand March from Aida. The music Italian, the uniforms French, the marching German, the palace Spanish. Again it was only flesh and blood that recalled the Incas: under the polished helmets of the guards were brown faces with the black eyes and slanting cheekbones of the Incas.

Inside the palace came another piece of that unselfconscious behaviour which for me is one of the attractions of South America. Before meeting the president we wanted to film the Palace Guard. The guard commander was sitting behind an ancient desk in a darkly panelled room. What light there was was reflected in his gleaming jackboots and in the plumed silver helmet on the desk beside him. His face — pale and Spanish — was almost lost behind a black moustache. The fustiness of his office spoke of red tape and of lethargic bureaucracy and of the due processes of the Peruvian military. It seemed unlikely that permission to film would be easily given here. But the moment we explained what we wanted, the face behind the moustache lit up. 'Me? You wish to film me with my men? Of course, of course!' And, with a childish pleasure which he felt perfectly free to show, he was on his feet sending messages to his troops to get ready, and calling his batman to give an extra polish to his already dazzling helmet. His was a spontaneity that we saw often in the Spanish Americans. Feelings, whether of pleasure or displeasure, are often freely shown. They're not, as tends to happen in the Anglo-Saxon world, suppressed in order to keep up an image of dignity, poise, and invulnerability.

We finished filming the Palace Guard and took leave of them with smiles and handshakes, and then it was time for our audience with the head of state. As on the outside of the palace, so on the inside. Everything was European, no trace of Indian. The walls of the ante-room were faced with Spanish tiles, the seats we waited on were carved with designs from Castile. It was as though the Incas had never existed.

A door opened and in a flurry of equerries and epauletted aides de camp we were introduced to President Fernando Belaunde Terry. Moving briskly along a corridor to the state room designated for the interview I began outlining the areas I hoped to discuss with him — the relegation of the Incas' descendants to Lima's slums, the failure of modern Peru to feed and house its people as Inca Peru had done. He put his hand on my arm and murmured, 'Peru is an old country, you know. I'm not responsible for everything that's wrong'. Mentally I added 'witty' to the description I had been given of this veteran of South American politics. I knew that he was a patrician who'd been democratically elected, then ousted in an army coup, then reinstated; he'd once fought a duel; he'd been shut in an island prison because of his views and had tried to escape by swimming; he'd been exiled and earned a living in the United States lecturing on architecture; he could speak without notes by the hour; an orator, a statesman, a survivor, but above all, they said, Belaunde was an architect, and it was in new roads and new towns that he saw the future of his country. Too much so, they said; he was obsessed by architecture.

Now we were seated on gold chairs in a gilded hall and the interview was underway. Was it not perplexing to the president that he could not feed his people as his predecessor The Inca had done? It was. He admired much in the Incas' old world. They had not used money, they had no international debt! And, of course, their rulers had far more powers than a modern democratic leader to organise and direct the state for its own good. And what about those slums which ringed his capital with shacks? What hope was there for the modern Incas who had nowhere else to exist? At that the architect emerged. Aides were sent off down the long hall to fetch maps, plans, architects' models, and the president was suddenly on his feet, pointer in hand to explain his vision of Peru. Hope for the slums? No, really there was none. The cities had grown too big to be saved. The future lay here — and his pointer was beyond the Andes on the great jungle belt of the Peruvian Amazon. New roads! New cities, there! That was the answer for Peru. We must expand into the jungle. The city slums where the Indians lived would never be more than slums. Never.

We left the capital and went up into the Andes again. To Pisac where the Incas had carved the sides of a great valley into fertile terraces and put a fortress above to protect them. Just below the ruins of that fort a small figure was bent over the maize crop. His name came from the Spaniards: Nicolas. But everything else about him — his almost Tibetan features, his stocky physique, his Quechua language, even the foot plough stuck in the earth beside him — everything else came from the Incas. Nicolas's life was not very different from that of his ancestors under the Incas. A life ordered by sun, rain and soil — the life of a peasant. In Europe Breughel was painting lives like Nicolas's in the sixteenth century.

Men like Nicolas still use the llama for transport as the Incas did. They still chew coca leaves for stamina and to deaden hunger. It's a life idyllic to look at, backbreaking to live.

Under the Incas Nicolas's life would have been a little easier. The terrace where he grows his maize would have yielded more maize then and of better quality, but now the old Inca irrigation culverts have fallen in, and in modern Peru there isn't the Inca labour force of virtual slaves to maintain them. And under the Incas Nicolas would never have worried about hunger; provided he worked as he was told, that would have been taken care of in the Inca welfare state. Two of Nicolas's three cows died this year and, at sixty, he is getting to an age when he won't have the strength to go on working. In Inca times old age would have held few fears because he'd have known that he'd be fed and housed in his retirement, but nowadays to stop working may mean to stop eating. With nothing to sell or barter at the local market, he could find himself in trouble. His sons and daughters have all gone off to live in those slums around Lima — something they wouldn't have been permitted to do in Inca times when the state controlled all movements.

The fact is underlined by the Inca gateway through which Nicolas, bent double under sheaves of corn, passes on his way up from the terrace. The gateway was once a checkpoint, part of a system of control which enabled the state to know where everyone was and even, if it chose, to uproot whole communities and send them off to develop remote corners of the Inca empire. I thought of the president in his palace the day before and of how much more easily he might achieve his goals if, like an Inca ruler, he could simply order the people of his swollen cities to migrate into the jungle and build new homes.

(Above) Peasant life —
idyllic to look at, back-
breaking to live, and almost
unchanged since Inca
times.

(Left) The Incas fed everyone. Now there are too
many mouths to feed.

(Above right) The land they
are leaving in the migration
to the cities.

(Below right) Cuzco
Cathedral. The Inca flag
against Spanish walls.

Old Nicolas, hobbling beneath his sheaves of corn, left the Inca gateway behind and approached his home. Outside the mud-walled little cottage his wife, Estefa, sat waist-deep in corn cobs as bright as beaten gold under the fierce mountain sun. She was doggedly picking the corn from the cobs. There seemed to be enough to keep her busy for several lifetimes. A pig squealed from somewhere behind a bank of flowers down the hillside and further below stretched the Sacred Valley of the Incas, winding along the river past the sites of Inca garrisons, townships, granaries and staging posts for their troops. Watching old Nicolas and Estefa in their idyllic setting there was a temptation to idealise them, to picture them actually as Incas still living in our country. But it was a day-dream. True, Nicolas and Estefa's life, except for the important fact that they have no guarantee against hunger, is little different from the peas-ant drudgery of their Inca ancestors. But, disappointingly, neither Nicolas or Estefa knows much about the mighty Incas. Asked about the three commandments of the Incas, they looked blank. In modern written Quechua those commandments are: *'Ama sua, ama llula, ama quella'* which translates as 'Don't lie, don't steal, don't be lazy'. But no one had ever told Nicolas and Estefa about that. To them the Inca identity means almost nothing. The past stretches back no further than their grand-parents.

We had come to find out what was happening to the Incas and so far the answers had been disappointing. Here in the country they were living amongst Inca ruins but these meant little to them; in the slums of the cities they were too busy surviving in their cardboard shacks ever to think much about their heritage. From all that we'd managed to discover so far it seemed that being Inca today amounts to nothing more than some wishful thinking at a folk festival.

How had an empire, a people, a culture as formidable as the Incas' been reduced to that? What had happened? The short answer was 'Pizarro'. On horseback we began to follow some of the paths of victory once taken by the Spaniard who had so improbably crushed an empire. He had arrived in the midst of the Incas with no more than one hundred and fifty men. From the start they were absurdly outnumbered and impossibly successful. The *conquistadores* had come to South America for gold and they would endure almost anything to get it. They were the sort of men who would have a wounded leg amputated in the field with a red hot sword and then ride on, rather than give up the quest. Pizarro's band had carried the search further than before, and by the time the Incas allowed him to find them, he was cut off from support and an easy prey. But he had two great advantages: the Incas were fatally divided in a civil war, and the Spaniards, armoured with Toledo steel and mounted on horseback, were the most effective soldiers in the Renaissance world. The Incas were still fighting in the Bronze Age. And on foot.

Pizarro and his hundred and fifty men, despite soiling themselves in terror as that scribe amongst them has noted, were all effrontery and audacity. Within days of arriving at the Inca city of Cajamarca they set the tone for the whole conquest of the Indians when they charged into an Inca army to kill seven thousand men in one afternoon and capture the

(Overleaf) Corpus Cristi — festival with Inca undertones — and three raucous days of music, drinking and dancing.

king, Atahuallpa. They exploited him, then they murdered him; they stabbed and burned and cheated their way through the empire to the city which, to the Incas, was literally the centre of the universe — Cuzco. There, despite the massive fortress of Sacsahuaman, they managed to loot and plunder a path through palaces and shrines, never hesitating to torture and kill, always in search of one thing — gold. The Incas called gold 'Sweat of the Sun'; silver was 'Tears of the Moon'. It was that sweat and those tears, so highly prized abroad, which eventually gave South America its fatal reputation as the land of Eldorado, turning it into a magnet which for four and a half centuries has drawn invaders intent on taking away its riches — from the first *conquistadores* to the latest multinationals.

The Spaniards' conquest of South America was swift. They tied up much of the continent in less than fifty years. But that doesn't mean they met no resistance from the Incas and the other native Indians. A day's ride from Cuzco along the Sacred Valley looms the terraced fortress of Ollantaytambo, and here one of the Incas' most stubborn leaders, Manco Inca, made a stand. You can sit now on the stone walled terraces, look down on the open square of land hundreds of metres below which is the only easy approach for an attacker, and imagine the scene. The Spaniards had sent one of Pizarro's brothers to crush the Incas, but the *conquistadores* were in for a surprise. A priest who was with them wrote afterwards, 'We tried to creep in at dawn and surprise the Incas, but it was a horrifying sight! As soon as we came within bow shot thousands of eyes were upon us and dark figures rose up above all the ramparts'. Manco Inca had manned the terraces with bowmen from the Amazon forests and with Inca troops armed with slingshots and javelins. And when the horrified Spaniards tried to retreat, Manco diverted the river Patacancha to flood the low ground, so their horses bogged down.

But no Inca withstood the *conquistadores* for very long. The empire was subjugated. Oppression became the order of the day, and the exploitation and destruction of the Incas commenced. Some estimates say that in the first fifty years under their Spanish masters so many Indians died from diseae and from slaving in the mines and on the land that their population fell by eighty per cent.

In Cuzco now you can watch a group of Indians kneeling on the pavement around a priest. A few hold small candles in the cold evening air. They are silent, submissive, so patient you could weep. At such moments it is easy to forget that their ancestors had been great conquerors themselves before the Spanish came, and easy to think of the defeated Incas only as wretched victims of invaders alien beyond their comprehension. As one of the considerable number of Spaniards who finally turned against the exploitation of the Incas wrote: 'The Spaniard and the Indian are dramatically opposed: The Indian is by nature without greed, the Spaniard is extremely greedy; the Indian is phlegmatic, the Spaniard is excitable; the Indian is humble, the Spaniard arrogant; the Indian is deliberate in all he does, and the Spaniard quick in all he wants, the Spaniard liking to order, the Indian hating to serve'. But, as elaborate Spanish architecture rose up on top of stolid Inca walls, the

conquered Indians did keep a certain Inca identity alive. When the conquerors banned a procession in which the Incas traditionally paraded the mummified bodies of their kings, and ordered them instead to carry statues of the Catholic saints, the Indians hid their mummies under the saints and paraded them anyway. Today in the main square of Cuzco you can still see that procession at Corpus Cristi, and though Saint Christopher and Saint John probably no longer have Atahuallpa and Manco Inca concealed under their robes, the square is a place to reflect on how, despite centuries of repression, a certain Inca pride still does survive. It was in this square that the Spanish beheaded one of the first Inca rebels, the King Tupac Amaru. That was in 1572, and two centuries later Inca spirit rose and was crushed here again when Tupac Amaru's great-great-great-grandson was executed after another unsuccessful revolt. At that time the Inca descendants were considered such a threat as to help loosen Spain's hold on its whole South American empire, so this Tupac Amaru the Second was made a warning to others — in the square in Cuzco the Spanish had him torn apart between four horses. But martyrdom feeds a cause, of course, and today, two centuries later, in that same square you may see evidence that the yearning for the Inca identity still exists: there are posters advertising 'Tupac Amaru — the Film'.

That Indian yearning for some return to greatness might have made progress one hundred and fifty years ago when Spain finally did lose her South American empire, but in fact the change made little difference to the Indians. Power passed not to them but to those South American-born descendants of the Spanish who had now thrown out the rule of Madrid in a wave of independence wars. Only the top of the pyramid changed. Orders that had once come from Spain now came from Quito, from Lima, from the presidents of the newly independent nations. But below them the landowners and the mine owners were mostly the same men as before, and the Indians remained 'their' Indians. Landowners like the Marquesses of Valleumbrosa, whose once palatial estate we saw lit by a symbolically setting sun in a valley between two black walls of mountains, kept their powers. Right up until the 1960s their Indians were held in a feudal grip — if an Indian didn't show up for work one Sunday he could be whipped; if one of his owner's cows died while the Indian was shepherding it, he could be made to replace it; if his wife was raped by the landowner there wasn't much he could do about it. The Inca identity remained as repressed as it had been throughout the previous three hundred years of colonial rule.

Then in the 1960s came what looked like a new dawn — not some Inca messiah but a left-wing military government intent on giving the land back to the people. The landowners were thrown out, Peru had a modern French Revolution, the estates became co-operatives. But now, a quarter century after that revolution, even though the big estates are long broken up and though cows graze in the dining hall of the Marquess of Valleumbrosa, and even though many Indians have parcels of land of their own, there is still no return to that security which the Incas enjoyed — security against hunger. One Spanish South American patronisingly explained this by saying that giving land to the Indians has been like giving seed to a barren woman. But the Indians have shown that they can coax rich yields from their small patches of land. What is missing is a government with a genius comparable to that of the ancient Incas for organising and co-ordinating the nation's agriculture.

For the descendants of the Incas it has all been the old story of Indian-meets-whiteman. The Apache, the Sioux, the Cheyenne, the Mayas, the Aztecs, the Incas. They probably all share the same family tree; they certainly share the same experience.

From that experience the descendants of the Incas are left with what? Many have gone down to the new slums round the cities — they have joined the urban drift which has seen country people leaving the land in many parts of the underdeveloped world in the last twenty years; many others are still living as peasants, and for them life is probably not much different from what was in Inca times, except that it is less secure; and a few are dreaming of an Inca revival.

Above the Incas' old southern capital of Cuzco, in the ruins of their vast fortress Sacsahuaman, we watched a pageant modelled on the Incas' Festival of the Sun. It was a fine pageant. The maize beer flowed amongst families perched on the magnificent ruins all around, ranks of the Peruvian army dressed as Inca warriors wheeled and clashed on the grassy mound between the walls, the 'Inca King' watched from his throne and the 'High Priest' raised the ceremonial knife above the sacrificial llama. It was a good day. Spirits were high, there were signs of enthusiasm among the Indians, back-slapping and laughter among the soldiers, camera-clicking among the tourists, and proud words from the Inca 'nobles': 'I *am* Inca,' the school master who had won the role of the King had told me outside the arena, 'And every day I feel more Inca. That I am conscious of being Inca is something which affects everything I do!' Borne on a litter, attired in the golden armour of the Son of the Sun, he clearly believed that Inca identity is more than just a daydream. And I would like to have believed with him. But the truth seemed to lie all around us. The walls of the once great Inca fortress were ruined walls, slab tumbled on slab, boulder on boulder. They spoke too eloquently of what has really happened to the Incas.

A CONTINENT CRUCIFIED?

CHAPTER 2

In the catacombs beneath the church of San Francisco in Lima, that city founded by Pizarro as his capital, skulls stare down at you from dusty shelves, and up at you from kiln-shaped burial chambers beneath your feet. These are the Lima people of past centuries. They have no headstones, no identification, nothing to distinguish between white and black and Indian, between clerk and beggar, between the blameless and the wicked. But because this is South America there is one thing that we *do* know about all those anonymous citizens of the past: they all died Roman Catholics. For centuries most South Americans have been baptized and married and buried in The Faith. South America is imbued with Catholicism. Nine out of ten children are still baptized into Mother Church, and it is estimated that by the end of this century more than half the Catholics of the world will be Latin Americans. Until recently the Roman Catholic Church has been the single most influential institution in the continent. How has it used that influence? And how is it using it now? ¶Climbing worn brick steps from the catacombs you come up into the misty Lima sunlight in the old church's cloisters. Leaning columns and cracked arches speak of four hundred and fifty years of the Church in South America. Catholicism has been there so long that it is impossible to imagine how South American history might have been without it.

The cloisters are cracked and crazed by earthquake shocks. They remind you that, though the Spanish conquerors are long gone, the Church they brought with them, though battered and changed, remains.

(Page 32) Penitence in Quito's Holy Week.

The Church arrived with the *conquistadores,* and in the main squares of many cities you can see that it was regarded as central from the beginning. Typically, when Pizarro founded Lima the first buildings to be planned were the Church and the *ayuntamiento* — the administration building. Sited close together, they were the twin centres of power — the secular and the sometimes but not always spiritual. Here on earth the Church had to serve two masters, the King and the Pope. Sometimes the Church served the King: there was nothing immediately spiritual in the role of the priest who was with Pizarro on the day when his small force of Spaniards set a trap for the mighty Atahuallpa and the Incas. As the *conquistador* and the Inca met for the first time it was the priest who stepped forward and provoked Atahuallpa by delivering to him not the respectful gifts he was accustomed to receiving from visitors, but a mere piece of paper which would have informed him, if by some miracle he had been able to read, that he must bow to the supreme rule of Charles V and of the Pope. Predictably the Inca treated the disappointing 'gift' with contempt, and the priest, having helped engineer Atahuallpa's insult to the Pope and the Spanish king, stood back and watched it avenged as Spanish horsemen charged from their hiding places and carried out their famous slaughter of some seven thousand Incas. And today, if you're looking for a symbol of how the Church and the State were often united, there is the body (they say) of Pizarro himself lying like a saint in a glass-sided tomb in the cathedral: the ruler who went forward to open the veins of South America honoured by the Church which grew rich with him.

But if that is how it was, with the priests hand in glove with the conquerors, then how did the Church win the trust and the support of so many of the poor and the oppressed? Part of the answer to that can be seen on the tomb of the man whose discovery of the Americas opened the way for both the conquerors and the Church. On the island of Santo Domingo, carved on the tomb of Columbus (or 'Colon' as he is in Spanish) is a panel showing a priest holding back the *conquistadores* and shielding the Indians. This is the Dominican Friar Bartolome de las Casas. When las Casas first went to the new world he accepted the widespread abuse of the Indians and their exploitation as virtual slaves of the conquerors. But eventually he was sickened by the floggings and the killings to the point where he turned and became South America's first great rebel priest. He turned on both his church and on the state and began to argue for the conquered and the downtrodden. His advocacy was strong enough to reach Madrid and to trouble the Court. Indeed there came a time when the Court became so concerned over the sufferings of its new subjects in the expanding Spanish empire that serious consideration was given to suspending all further colonisation — a moral hiccough which must be unique in the annals of imperialism. What government of any other growing empire ever seriously questioned its own right to take over as much of the globe as it could? The Moghuls? The Romans? The Dutch? The British?

De las Casas the Spaniard was the pioneer of humanitarianism in the South American Church, and to this day he has always had sufficient heirs in spirit to keep the Church divided between God and Mammon. Later we planned to meet some of those heirs, the rebel priests of today, but first we wanted to learn more about the other side of the Church — the establishment side.

In the cathedral in Lima in the side chapel which houses Pizarro in his glass-sided tomb were a few tourists. Among them an Indian stood, shoulders hunched under his coloured blanket, gazing at those remains — all clawing ribs and flesh like smoked bacon. I went over to the Indian: 'What do you think about Pizarro?' With the resignation of centuries he told me, 'Well, he destroyed our way of life of course, but that's what conquerors do. And he did bring us God.'

How had the Church won over the Indians? Wouldn't they have seen it as just another arm of the white giant who was crushing them? Their own gods and temples were torn down, men who'd worshipped the sun were left, as Stanley Reynolds once put it, with mere candles.

The Indians were pushed into the conquerors' Church in uncom-prehending millions by missionaries often more interested in numbers than in ideals. In just one day during the conquest of Mexico fourteen thousand Indians were 'converted'. What 'converted' meant to any Indian was that he was read — in Spanish which he didn't understand — a theological tract, he watched a mass, and was baptized. It was a veneer of Catholicism applied by a Church which often supported the enslave-ment of the Indian and his family and drummed it into him that it was God's will that he should be poor and ignorant. It was a doctrine which kept the Indians down and served both State and Church, because it was Indian labour, especially in the mines, that helped make both rich. The Church even *owned* mines. And it is estimated that more than eight million Indians died in the mines of Peru alone.

Some horrid exhibits in a Lima museum prompted the thought that perhaps the infamous Spanish Inquisition had been the key to 'convert-ing' the Indians. In the museum a life-sized model lay on the rack, his mouth silently shrieking; another's face twisted as his feet were coated with oil and held by a brazier; another lay pop-eyed as a hooded inquisitor forced water into his nose and mouth. If our picture of the old Catholic Church needed any more blackening, then this was the paint. The Holy Inquisition had done its worst for three hundred years in Spain and for two hundred and fifty years in South America to impose con-formity, to make sure that no-one questioned the way things were run.

But the Inquisition exerted no direct pressure on the Indians. They were exempt from its attentions. To assume that it played any part in the subjugation of the Indians would be to be misled by a historic smear campaign which has greatly exaggerated the Inquisition's scope. Over the years, since Drake saved England from the Spanish fleet, Protestant historians have done a thorough job of blackening the image of Spanish Catholicism. They have created a lie that has become known as 'The Black Legend'. They have selected the facts which suited their theme and suppressed others. They haven't told us, for example, that the

(Above and right)
The Indians were seen as
virgin souls, ripe for
conversion. Ecuador.

(Left) So, later, were the
slaves. Ecuador.

English burned more Catholics in the reign of Elizabeth I alone than the entire deathroll of heretics burned by the Inquisition during three whole centuries. In Lima only thirty people were ever burned for their religious beliefs and of them most were luckless British sailors; none was Indian. Indeed in 1537 the Pope himself had come out on the side of the poor and the oppressed and had decreed that Indians were to be regarded not as animals but as human beings who possessed souls, and therefore were not to be enslaved and deprived of liberty. But there is an old saying in South America to the effect that while to acknowledge such orders and decrees is essential, to obey them may not be, and even though the racks and thumbscrews of the Inquisition were not used to convert the Indians, the mere presence of the swords and pikes of the conquerors cannot have failed to add weight to the preaching of the missionaries. And those preachings themselves contained a powerful inducement to conversion — the threat of eternal torment in hell for anyone who resisted. There is an alarming painting of those torments, done in glowing tones of hellfire red, which covers a substantial section of wall in the Campañia Church in Quito. To watch Indians pondering the demons which are emasculating adulterers with fiery pincers and disembowelling gluttons is to be reminded of one fact that must be put on the scales in any attempt to decide how much South America has been crucified by the Church and how much the continent has gained. The Church thrust guilt and fear of hellfire onto the native South Americans. Few of them had probably ever been entirely free of it, but the Church honed guilt into a knife which could be twisted to manipulate men. Quite recently a missionary to a newly discovered group of Indians in the Amazon was recorded saying, 'Do you know that when we arrived these people actually had no word for "guilt". We've had to invent one for them and teach them what it means'.

We had to come up to Quito in Ecuador for what is really a great festival of guilt. On Good Friday a long procession of penitents trudges around the city, bowed down under wooden crosses, hoping to expiate the sins of the past year. During Holy Week in Quito religious feeling swells up, finally to overflow from the churches down into the streets in a tide of purple-hooded penitents on the Friday. It was Monday now and already there was fervour in the air. I turned away from the hell red painting of future torments and moved further into the church to where an Indian mother stood suckling her baby and gazing ardently at a painted wooden Virgin Mary. Others were kneeling in rapt prayer.

Indians appear to pray differently from more sophisticated people. Their faces seem suffused with faith — with a poignant dependance on the god of their old conquerors. Above the praying Indians the wall of the church shimmered with beaten gold. Gold had played its part in drawing priests to these far regions. But a greater attraction must have been the Indians: millions of souls to be converted — naive, willing converts.

Outside the church we met up with one of our team, Marc, fuming. Marc, as camera assistant, had gone to our van to fetch a tripod, and coming back through a crowded street-market he had discovered that not everyone in the city was overcome with the Holy Week spirit of repentence. As he was wading through the crowd with the tripod held on his shoulder, Marc found himself pressed on from all sides by Indians who barely came up to his armpits. As they pressed and milled around his ribs, he felt his wallet being removed from his jeans.

Now Marc is a strong man, a Karate black-belt with a physique that had earned him in our group the unquestioned responsibility of lifting up a corner of the van whenever a wheel needed changing. And Marc, when he felt himself being robbed by midgets, began to struggle. But he couldn't throw down the tripod to set his hands free for fear of damaging it, and the more he thrashed and tried to kick, the more his small captors pressed around him and lifted him off the ground.

By the time they let him down, the wallet had gone and so had a pair of sunglasses, and he was left steaming with frustration. 'I got hold of two of them', Marc told us, 'picked them up and shook 'em, but the one who had the wallet had already got away'. And he pronounced on the city his accolade of disapproval, 'Quito sux!'

His disgust wouldn't last though, because in Marc a sense of humour always reasserted itself, but a few minutes later we were all inclined to agree with him when we came under a hail of maize and small potatoes for trying to film Indian traders in the street-market. *Gringos* aren't always welcome, especially when the white-skinned intruders have cameras. Ducking under a light hail of potatoes, which I remembered had originally been one of the Andean Indians' gifts to the world, we reached a covered section of the market where, on a platform above

(Below) San Francisco Monastery, HQ of Quito's Holy Week.

(Left) With a cactus cross across his back and shackles on his feet — this Quito penitent turns guilt into masochism...

(Above) There may be smiles under some of the hoods...

(Right) And even children enjoy the day...

(Far right) But self punishment predominates, and the crosses are almost too heavy to lift.

decks of melons, oranges, beans, corncorbs and fish, stood a carved Christ crowned with thorns and shouldering a cross. This was *Jesus del Gran Poder,* the Jesus of Great Power who is the inspiration of Quito's Holy Week.

He had been only an obscure version of the deity, standing in an unfrequented corner of Quito's San Francisco church, until the 1960s. His rise to prominence began when someone reported that a prayer to the Christ for a cure had been answered. Soon more cures were reported and replicas of the carved Christ began to be made. The cures multiplied and *Jesus del Gran Poder* became the centre-piece of the Ecuadoreans' Good Friday. A society of pentitents was formed around him and the procession as it is today took shape.

Now, this replica of the adored figure stood above the prayers and hymns of the market people in a service presided over briskly but with feeling by a short Franciscan friar with horn-rimmed glasses and a balding head. As always during Holy Week, Father Jorge (George) Henriquez was in a hurry. He'd just finished his daily broadcast on Radio Jesus of Great Power from the studio in the old church's tower, soon he would be having the tenth meeting that week at the *Alcaldia* — the mayor's office — to arrange details of the big day.

In the down-to-earth cheerful way which Franciscans often have, Father Henriquez has been running Quito's rather masochistic Holy Week for years now. As we followed him out through the street market, energy seemed to buzz from under his coarse brown robe. His presence stayed the hands of the potato throwers and we followed him gratefully through the market stalls, up old steps that reeked of urine, and into the tranquil, cloistered garden of the San Francisco church. A chattering band of novices bustled along the cloister beneath paintings of Christ on the road to his crucifixion. Some had Indian faces, most were white, one was black. They passed through an arched doorway and out of sight leaving laughter in the air behind them. Soon, through a grill in the wall we heard their voices again, singing now in a sonorous chant. Father Henriquez led us past the tall palms in the cloistered garden and into the big church itself. As he went along, he gesticulated and vibrated with energy, stopping for a word here and a nod there with others involved in the staging of the coming Friday. Inside the church they were already starting to drag the pews aside to make a clear space. In front of the altar a specially built vehicle waited like a parked bus for the figure of Jesus of Great Power to be raised onto it that night, ready for the big procession the next day. Sunlight splashed from the high windows onto groups of Indians kneeling on the old warped timbers of the floor. Their eyes rested on saints and madonnas behind ranks of dripping candles. The wooden idols were garishly painted, with vermilion wounds. A dead Christ lay in his mother's arms. His own arms hinged at the shoulder so that he could be either spread for crucifixion or folded for this embrace. I reflected that the image of the crucifixion has been so often seen that it has lost impact, and this grand guignol version tended to turn away whatever feeling was left in me. How could one be moved by such a chamber of horrors? Then an Indian mother with a child in her arms stood beside Mary and her nailed son, and I found a lump in my throat. As Good Friday drew near the fervour, even hysteria, in the air could be contagious.

That fervour was present too across the cobbled square in Quito's cathedral at a service of black medieval intensity. As a dirge of rumbling chords and plaintive voices dripped from the high organ loft, eleven sombre black figures inched their way around the aisles in the cathedral gloom below. Each wore a black hood and cloak which trailed heavily behind him, and at the head of this grim procession went a great black flag with a red satin cross. You almost heard the crackling of Inquisition fires. Under each black cloak was one of the city's senior prelates, each representing one of the eleven disciples, each dragging a black cloak of sin towards the altar. As the *monseñores* hauled their black burdens slowly towards the altar, the congregation, far from being awed or reverent, dashed from one side of the nave to the other to get the best view. Today they saw the top men of the Church humbling themselves in unaccustomed self-abasement. Look! There was the Bishop, and here came the Cardinal, bowed under clouds of ignominy!

When this strangest of all Catholic rituals began in the sixteenth century, the public lowering of the mighty must have seemed even more extraordinary. The gap then between the heads of the Church and their flock was so wide as to make such public humiliation astonishing. The church leaders of those times were proud men, almost always Spanish born, usually of noble birth. The salary of an archbishop two hundred years ago could be as high as $160 000. Some became viceroys with the power of kings, and even though there were a few humble men amongst them like one bishop who learned the Indians' language and travelled to visit every village in his mountain diocese, the majority of those early prelates, as they sat on fine furniture in gilded palaces, must have felt themselves far nearer to God than to their flocks. In his novel of those times *The Bridge at San Luis Rey,* Thornton Wilder wrote of an Archbishop of Lima: 'The Archbishop knew that almost all the priests in the land were rogues. It required all his delicate epicurean education to prevent his doing something about it. He had to repeat over and over to himself his favourite notions — that the injustice and unhappiness in the world are a constant, that progress is a delusion, and that the poor, never having known happiness, are insensible to misfortune.'

The cloaked figures arrived at last in front of the altar and prostrated themselves — face down — eleven black stains on the pink carpet. The Cardinal, in white satin, drew the great black flag caressingly across their backs to end the service, and the congregation pressed forward for a chance to kiss his ring. Standing amongst them, pushed this way and that, I felt again that struggle between head and heart that had caught me in front of the dead Christ in his mother's arms: surely the whole service had been nothing more than a piece of theatre? But these people struggling now to kiss the ring — their humble longing brought the lump to my throat again. Late on the night before Good Friday we went to the San Francisco church to watch them raise Jesus of Great Power onto his carriage. Padre Henriquez had already gone to bed. That afternoon in the great church he had delivered a ringing sermon to an overflowing

(Left) Church and State —
sometimes allies,
sometimes enemies.

(Above) Religious souvenirs
— Quito, Good Friday.

(Right) In the fourth hour
of the procession.

(Below right) Quito is a city
of bells, domes and spires.

congregation, then he had joined a dozen of the brothers to carry the host to thousands of outstretched hands. Now, with months of organising over, he was asleep in the monastery waiting for the big day of his year.

Up behind the altar they were unbolting the Jesus of Great Power and lowering him carefully to the ground. He was dusty. A young girl tenderly wiped his painted face, two boys kissed his wooden robe. With ropes and pulleys they hoisted him above the carriage. He dangled from the church ceiling above an elevated platform on the carriage, where he would ride eight feet above the wheels. As he was lowered into place there was a great heaving and straining and the carriage threatened to capsize. We rushed to lend our shoulders, and catastrophe was averted. Jesus of Great Power was settled on his carriage and left alone in splendour until the morning. The church's lights were switched off and we all moved down the steps past sleeping beggars bundled in the church doorway, and out into the still night. In the morning Quito's pretty colonial squares were washed with pink sunlight. The cracked bells in the towers and domes of the churches clanged and shuddered out the news. This was the day. In the universe where God had made all things, in the world where the Pope commanded his vast following, in South America where nine out of every ten were Catholics, in Quito where the church had been unshakeably entrenched for four and a half centuries, this was the day.

And the South Americans were going to enjoy it. Anyone who imagined that, because the procession was about penitence, Quito was about to burst into tears of grief and recrimination was mistaken. The atmosphere in the big yard behind the church where the penitents were dressing was cheerful. Hundreds of men and a few women were putting on robes and tall pointed hoods, all in various shades of mauve and purple. As faces disappeared behind the masks below the peaked hoods (the *cucuruchus*) there was laughter. And even when only eyes could be seen behind the slits in the purple cloth, they mostly looked merry enough. Many had full-sized timber crosses, and penitents were testing the weight of theirs against others. Some had beams to carry across their shoulders. A few, but it was only a very few (and under Padre Henriquez's persuasion their number decreases each year), really intended to suffer. One had shackles on his ankles and a cross made of spiney cactus resting on his bare shoulders; another was whipping himself — not fiercely but enough to redden his back. But the mood, as they crowded through an echoing corridor down to the cloisters, was festive.

Inside the San Francisco church Jesus of Great Power waited on his carriage, the crowd milling below him. We caught a young pick-pocket with his fingers in our equipment bag; he went off into the congregation protesting his innocence. There were queues at the confessional where Indians knelt whispering into both sides of the box. Its door occasionally fell open to give a glimpse of a priest inside on a magenta cushion. One man in the queue moaned aloud, 'Hurry up. If I don't get it down now, I'll be damned for a year'.

Outside the church the beggars had been cleared from the big doorway. The town bandsmen stuck old clarinets between old teeth and set up a wail as the carriage began to emerge, with Jesus of Great Power shuddering against the sky as the wheels were eased down the steps. For half an hour the hooded penitents kept on emerging behind from the church, hood after hood after purple hood. Quito's Good Friday had begun.

For five hours the purple hoods laboured between banks of spectators, through narrow lanes, up past the park and the statue of Benalcazar the *conquistador* who had founded Quito, and then past Simon Bolivar the Liberator who had taken it from the Spanish. Every so often they halted to rest from their crosses and beams, while the thrown coins around the feet of Jesus del Gran Poder grew deeper.

By five o'clock it was raining — it always rains on Good Friday in Quito. And the first penitents were arriving back at the San Francisco cloisters. Hoods were pulled off, necks were stretched, 'Phew! Let's have a Coke!' Padre Henriquez had been leading the procession from a police car complete with red flashing lights and loud speaker. He emerged now to the expectant crowd outside his beloved San Francisco Church. From the top of the steps he led them in 'Three cheers for our Jesus of Great Power!' The shouted *'Vivas'* carried through the rain, the carriage arrived in the square, and with Jesus covered in a polythene sheet against the weather, it wobbled its way in through the big doors. The crowd pressed forward, mounted policemen rode into them to protect the Christ. Another Good Friday was over.

It had been moving and impressive, but really it was something of a fossil. Once upon a time there were great affirmations of faith like this one all over South America. The Church was strong. But by the nineteenth century times were changing. The Spanish viceroys had gone, new men were in power and the Church had to seek a new arrangement. Some churchmen tried to keep up their old close relationship with the state, but that meant siding with whoever was in power, be he democrat or (more likely) dictator. Other priests — the ones who had always sided with the downtrodden — wanted to build a more independent Church responsive to the cry of the people, but that meant losing the protection of the state.

Now those mounted policemen heading the crowds off from the Christ symbolised the dilemma perfectly. Ever since the nineteenth century the Church has been divided between either siding with the powerful on the one hand or with the weak and the poor on the other.

To see what it means for the Church to side with the poor we crossed the continent to Brazil, to the megalopolis of Sao Paulo. Now, as at any time in the last four and a half centuries, you can find priests who champion the poor in any country of South America. We chose Sao Paulo because it is one of the places where their conflict with the state has been most overt in recent years.

Sao Paulo is a pressure-cooker of a city: twelve or thirteen million people live there — no one has counted; they've increased by about half in just ten years; the number of jobs has not grown in proportion. When you learn that not long ago the state of Sao Paulo was producing more than all but sixteen *nations* in the world, you wonder how there can be poverty. There was talk of a 'Brazilian Miracle'. Whole schools of

(Left) Sao Paulo — poor.
(Below) Sao Paulo — rich.

economic theory grew up around it. But this is South America where the profits rarely filter down to the poor. The middle class benefitted — the number of homes with TV's and fridges doubled. But the poor got little: seventy per cent of Sao Paulo's homes have no drains; half have no piped water. In Sao Paulo you can see two countries: one is a rich, highly industrialised Belgium; the other a desperately poor India.

Holding down the lid was a military government. Often in South America such regimes have worked hand in hand with an obliging Church — the Generals and the Cardinal in crushing accord. But in Sao Paulo it was different. The Cardinal of Sao Paulo, instead of standing aside while the regime crucified the people, and instead of preaching nostrums about everything being better in the next life, attacked the generals with all his power. His stand has made him some bitter enemies within the Catholic Church — men who see him as neglecting the spiritual role of the Church and turning it into something that is little more profound than a political party. But to Cardinal Evaristo Arns, the Church, instead of being the opium of the people, had to become the defender of their rights.

We caught up with the Cardinal on his way to a poor district to preach at a Sunday service. His Volkswagen Beetle had broken down at the road side and he was bending over it in his black cassock and purple hat, trying to fix the fanbelt. His sermon today would be sure to contain a pointed attack on the government's failure to distribute the state's wealth. His chosen battleground with the government was now economics; he had already contributed to their defeat on human rights. To bring that about he had taken part in a long struggle. As early as 1960 when a Brazilian bishop had been tortured and threatened with expulsion, the Pope himself had told the military government, 'Whatever is done to that bishop is done to me'. Ten years later it was Arns' turn to challenge the torturers. When two of his priests were arrested and tortured because they'd campaigned for better pay for workers, the Cardinal ordered notices to be nailed to every church door in Sao Paulo describing what had happened. In the end, of course, it took more than denouncements on church doors to stop the atrocities. In fact the military's first reaction was to increase the torturing. Even children were included, and army officers were given torture lessons with live victims. By 1975 a Sao Paulo opinion poll showed that, while six people out of ten were afraid of violence from robbers, seven feared it from the police. It was fuel to the Cardinal's campaign. Every time a prisoner died under torture, Arns held a mass, sometimes in a cathedral ringed by tanks. At one mass six bishops and three thousand priests came to support him. Eventually the Military Governor of Sao Paulo was sacked and it was the beginning of the end of terror.

When Arns had first been appointed Cardinal he had up-ended the pyramid and sent his priests out to put their heads together with the people. He wanted the people to decide what it was that the Catholic Church should be doing in their vast and often appalling city. Not surprisingly one of the answers which came back was 'fight poverty'. Now we went to the slums to see some of Arns' priests at work.

(Below and right) Once they were Catholics, now they're Mormons. Otavaleño Indians, Ecuador.

50

Our guide to this ignored part of Sao Paulo, festering away almost within sight of the extravagant architecture of the business centre, was a priest from the United States. He was a man who had gone through a process of politicisation which must have been similar to the one experienced by Bartolome de las Casas, that first rebel priest of South America back in the sixteenth century. When Father Drexel had first arrived in Brazil twenty years ago, he had begun by accepting things as they were. Then it dawned on him that he never seemed to bury anyone over the age of forty, and at the same time he was noticing that while the government was spending huge sums on grandiose hydro-electric and nuclear schemes of doubtful value, almost nothing was ever spent on sewers, housing or schools.

In the three short years of its existence the slum where Drexel now lives and works has already filled a fair-sized cemetery. Shop owners hire killers to eliminate those kids whom they suspect of stealing. The police will round up dozens of kids and threaten beatings and electrodes unless someone confesses to the latest crime, acting on the assumption that if you're poor, you must be guilty.

Watching Father Drexel and his fellow priests trying to make life more possible for people born into such chains, you could not for a moment think of the Church as crucifying South America; clearly these priests were men of whom the original rebel, Bartolome de las Casas, would be proud. But neither could you hold back in discussion with them a doubt which arises in any non-Catholic's mind when faced with growing slums and a swelling population which outnumbers both the jobs and the local food supply: wasn't the Church contributing to the suffering by forbidding birth control? Asking the priests about that, I felt that they were in an unresolved dilemma, caught between the dictates of the Pope and the human evidence before their eyes. I cannot be sure of that. But to an outsider, unaffected by holy law, it did look as though the problem which these redoubtable and self-sacrificing priests were labouring to ease was a problem partly created by their own Church.

That is a dilemma of quite recent origin, but there is nothing new in the Church's finding itself split between the poor and the powerful. The Church has long managed to accommodate on the one hand priests who are content to accept whatever ruler may be in power and to concern themselves only with the spiritual side of their flock, and on the other hand priests like those in Sao Paulo who believe that it is idle to care for the spirit if the flesh is suffering starvation, privation, injustice. The division has always existed and has never seriously threatened the Church. But today there is another threat, and it is new. In Ecuador we watched missionaries at work amongst the admirable Otavalo Indians. The Indians of Otavalo are great survivors. They have been conquered by the Incas and by the Spaniards, they have been converted by the Catholics, they have absorbed the Incas' barter system and the capitalist world's monetary system, and they have remained unshakeably themselves. They are such good weavers that many now make a lot of money and sell internationally, but they always dress and live according to Otavalo custom, and they always live in their villages. You may meet an

(Above) Ex-Catholic Indian outside new Mormon church. Ecuador.

Otavaleño in his white trousers and blue cloak on a jet flying to New York to sell cloth, but you are very unlikely ever to meet him spending the profits from that sale on a house in a city.

And now the Otavaleños are absorbing another invasion. It is missionaries again, and to the Otavaleños that is no threat. They have absorbed western religion before, they have been Catholics for centuries. But for the Catholic Church the new missionaries do pose a threat, because they are not Catholics but protestants. And they are making considerable inroads.

Originally the Catholic Church was protected against such predations on its flocks. First the Inquisition and then Catholic-orientated governments made it impossible for other religions to intrude, let alone to compete. But now South America is a free for all, with Evangelists, Jehovah's Witnesses, Seventh Day Adventists sweeping down from the USA, Bibles in hand, to woo the once unquestioning followers of the Roman Church.

In Ecuador among the Otavaleños it was the Mormons whom we watched. And they were making steady progress. In a newly built Mormon church and medical centre the Indians, in their immaculate white trousers and black pigtails, were being converted from Catholicism to Mormonism at the rate of twenty every month. The dedicated young Mormon missionaries in their dark suits and ties stood in the hot Andean sun and told me with quiet confidence of their progress and their plans. They had been touring Indian villages with their film about how Christ visited South America, and the rate of baptism was growing. Theirs is the fastest growing church in South America. Which means that the Catholic Church must be the fastest shrinking. At the moment, of course, it is no more than a flea sucking blood from an elephant. The Catholic Church is vast in comparison to its new rivals. But they are gaining and it is losing. If things continue at this rate, it is the Catholic Church itself which will eventually be crucified — by its deserting South American flock.

BRAVO, BREAD AND CIRCUSES

CHAPTER 3

Journeying through South America has its difficulties on a physical level. There's enough red tape in some of the countries (with the notable exceptions of Colombia and Argentina) to tie up an arriving film team for a week. But, for one of our films, we wanted to make not so much a physical journey as a psychological one. We wanted to travel into the South American soul. To do that we would have to overcome a difficulty that was not physical but philosophical: we would have to find a way to penetrate the myths and stereotypes about the South Americans, and go deeper. We decided that the best signposts for such a journey would be three of the big stars whom the South Americans admire. By looking at the stars and their fans we might learn what it is that brings South Americans to their feet cheering, what are the qualitites they find inspiring, what it is, in fact, which fires their souls. ¶We began our search in Colombia, in the capital Bogota. In the old quarter you could almost have been in Spain: cobbled streets, heavy curved tiles on the roofs, wrought iron balconies, archways giving vignettes of courtyards filled with flowers and cool fountains. And to confirm the impression, a stone plaque outside one of those most Spanish-looking houses announcing it as the headquarters of the Colombian Hispanic Society. The district was evidence of centuries of South American admiration for — naturally enough — Spain.

As the great conquerors, the Spaniards had for centuries been the ones who set standards for the South Americans to aspire to, and it was the Spanish who introduced a sport whose stars could show us a good deal about what it is in a man that is considered admirable in South America. That sport was bullfighting.

The British Empire has left people playing cricket in far corners of the earth; the memorial of Spanish rule is bullfighting. Far from Spain, in Colombia, in Venezuela, in Peru and in Ecuador, all of which broke free from Spanish rule more than one hundred and fifty years ago, the bullfighter still embodies Spain. Indeed, bullfighting in South America has quite deliberately been made **more** Spanish. In a general movement to hold on to the influence of Spain, in the nineteenth century, Colombian aristocrats imported the 'suit of lights' and the ritual of what they still saw as the mother country in order to hispanicize the relatively crude bullfighting of the new world. I think that, to anyone who doubts that the brutality of the *conquistadores* in their conquest of South America was inherently Spanish, the answer is the bullfight. It confirms that blood and death are close to the Spanish soul. No other nations than Spanish-speaking ones still permit such mortal display; cockfighting, hunting, motor racing, even boxing may, in their different ways, be concerned with death, but only Spanish-speaking nations still pit a man against a powerful animal in a dance of death. There is a pool of blood and sorrow deep in the Spanish soul — something which Goya's paintings reveal, and which permeates South America.

To get started we had to find a bullfighter, an exponent of this Spanish tradition, and that was not easy. On our first attempt I had gone to a bullfight week in a small town of Colombia, with a Colombian film crew. We had been warned that the bullfighting fraternity could be hostile to foreigners, so we had made careful overtures. But a message I telexed back to headquarters in Sydney later shows that efforts at diplomacy did not succeed:

'**Colombia, January 28.** Progress report. Bullfight film off to a rocky start. During our first five days of attempted filming, the cameraman had a fever, I had the runs, the bullfighter's manager went back on six months of promises and denied us access unless we signed over the ABC's budget for the next decade, the Mayor's office delayed our passes, the banks held on to our funds, air bookings failed with the local computer caput, and swarms of would-be presenters joined in whenever I tried to speak direct to camera. An average week's filming. But then we had a problem — complete camera failure!' It had been a debacle, ending in a final day of humiliation when the all-powerful bullfight manager had summoned us to his hotel, dictated to us the terms of an agreement financially more appropriate to the filming and selling of 'Ben Hur' than of a documentary, and ordered us to have it typed and to bring it to him for signature. '*Por supuesto, señor*', I had said through gritted teeth, 'Of course, sir. And where will we find you?'

'I'll be somewhere on the beach'. And he had swaggered off. He was as unpleasant an example of vindictive Latin machismo as you could hope to find, and we were in his power. Either we did as he demanded or

(Page 54) A would-be star. Palenque, Colombia.

we got no film and wasted the trip. We typed the agreement. Then we walked the crowded beach. Our sweat ran down our arms and on down the agreement, our feet burned in the sand, and what seemed like several million sunbathing Colombians must have wondered why we peered down at their faces so desperately. We never found our man on the beach and our attempt to film ended in failure. Latin macho had triumphed over *gringo* enthusiasm.

But later, in Bogota, we had more luck. A Sunday of bullfighting was scheduled, with a card that underlined not only the South American connection with Spain, but also the disenchantment — the love-hate of a former colony for the imperial power. On the bill were two Spanish *toreros* but only one South American. It was a sore point with the locals; already that season there had been protests that the Spanish were taking over South American bullfighting and this was a further insult to the courage and competence of Colombia. The lone South American who now had the task not just of killing two bulls but also of doing far better than his two Spanish competitors was a home-town boy, Jairo Antonio Castro from Bogota. We found him in the empty bullring practising. Jairo Antonio's friend and helper, Manuel, was charging at him with a pair of authentic horns mounted on a bicycle wheel. Jairo Antonio, as he flexed and turned under the attack, was becoming the epitome of grace under pressure — the words which Hemingway, after watching bullfighters, had used to define all courage. We saw then, and we would see again when the bullfighter faced real bulls, the irresistible study of arrogance, exhibitionism and cool courage which a man — or for that matter a woman — must show if he is to satisfy the desire of a bullfight crowd. No-one could mistake the signals in the hips thrust extravagantly forward, the shoulders proudly back to lift the head high, the eyes and mouth cool to the point of contempt.

This machismo was echoed less theatrically in a hundred faces in the bullfight cafe where Jairo Antonio took us to discuss plans for filming. Everyone in the cafe had something to do with the coming *corrida,* and all were men. Even the old men had about them an air of knowing how to handle themselves which reminded me of men from the world of boxing. But here there was a certain extra stiffening of pride — the pride required for this most macho of all contests. Away from the bullring our *torero* was relaxed and warm. I shuddered at a photograph of his last *cornada* when a horn had ripped the side of his throat open just as he went in to kill. He had finished the kill, 'naturally' he explained, and then had been helped off towards the waiting needle and thread. I thought of the fighter I had seen tossed earlier in the year: suddenly he had been ten or fifteen feet above the ground, to come down backwards onto the sand and be trampled by the bull. They had started to carry him off, unconscious, but the wounded fighter had come round, pushed them aside and come back, bleeding and torn, to the centre of the ring. There he had mastered the animal in a display of courage that had us all on our feet. There is, I thought then, no contest that is such a test of courage as the bullfight, and it tells us something of the South Americans that many of them have such an *aficion* — such a passion for it.

(Above) Jairo Antonio
Castro practising with a
cow.

(Left) Jairo Antonio's fan
club. Bogota, Colombia.

(Above right) This is to
South America what cricket
is to Australia — a colonial
legacy.

(Centre right) With one of
Jairo Antonio's victims.

(Below right) Jairo Antonio
triumphant.

To learn more of what the bullfight meant to its *aficionados* I became a member of Jairo Antonio's fan club. One of the things it meant, as with most bands of sports supporters, was plenty of drinking. Wherever we *aficionados* went in our red berets and white sweaters, the wine-skins were always raised above parted lips — theirs eager, mine protesting. Under a sloshing stream of sweet yellow wine, bullfighting seemed likely to become a blur. But by the time the Sunday of the *corrida* arrived, I had learned to drink from a wine-skin without spilling quite all of it and, more important, I had learned to say no.

The *aficionados*, on their way to the bullring, were rowdy and boisterous. The bullfighter, dressing in his hotel room with his team, was grave and quiet. I was reminded of a priest dressing for mass. Satins trimmed with gold were drawn tightly over the body that would soon be offered to the bull. The clothes were elaborate and restricting — certainly not what you would ideally choose for fighting a fast and dangerous animal. They could only be explained as part of a ritual. And the ritual of the bullfight seldom changes; it is as constant as high mass. I remembered that the bullfight had once been introduced to Italy, by the Borgias. But it had been thrown out as a pagan threat to the Roman Church. It seems that, for the Latin soul, the bullfight has some spiritual significance that is beyond anything you expect to find in a sport.

But there was little that was spiritual about Jairo's fan club by the time we had reached the bullring. Seated in our red berets, we formed a vociferous scarlet crescent on the terraces above the circle of sand. One after another self-appointed cheer-leaders would leap up to exhort our cheers for Jairo Antonio who today would surely demonstrate the superiority of South America in general and of Colombia in particular over the Spanish. The bullfighting equivalents of a football supporter's '2...4...6...8... Who do you appreciate' were spluttered out between great sucks of manzanilla from the inescapable wine-skins. Down below us, underneath the stands, Jairo Antonio had arrived and was kneeling in the chapel before the Virgin of Macarenas, patroness of bullfighters; the picadors were thumping their lances against a wall to fix the points; and the first bull was rushing through a tunnel towards the cell from which he would be released into the ring for an ordeal he could not guess at.

From a catwalk above the cell a barbed rosette was plunged down into the animal's shoulder. Infuriated he found a door opening in front of him, infuriated he charged. And there on the bright sand the bull saw — for the first time in his life — a man on foot. The bull charged and the ancient ritual began. The first *torero* to fight was not the Colombian, Jairo Antonio, but the more senior of the two Spaniards. Then came the second Spaniard. Their performances were sound but not inspiring. When Jairo Antonio's turn came, the welcoming roars of *'Viva Colombia, Viva Jairo Antonio'* soon gave way to sonorous *'Oles'* of deep pleasure as he settled skilfully into the old dance of death. He wheeled and turned, and provoked and challenged. He was as formal as a priest, as graceful as a dancer, as fearless as a statue. And because he was South American the crowd loved it all the more.

Watching those dark South Americans taking such pleasure in their *corrida,* I thought of how, a few hundred kilometres away, in the Caribbean, eleven descendants of slaves were preparing to travel to Australia in order to hurl a small leather missile at three pieces of wood defended by a man with another piece of wood. The British had enthused their empire with a sport which reflected what they perhaps admired in themselves. Cricket was aggressive yet politely restrained and impeccably fair. But Spain had bequeathed blood, ritual and death. You could not imagine the souls of these *aficionados* in the Bogota bullring being stirred by cricket.

By the time the bull went down under Jairo Antonio's flying charge with the sword, it was clear that the South American had done what his people desired: he had displayed great courage and self control; in adversity he had been not merely graceful, but arrogant as well; and, as a bonus, he had outperformed their former lords and masters — the Spaniards.

But to fight bulls is still to emulate the Spanish — even if you sometimes manage to do it better than they do, it stops short of defying them. But there is in the South Americans a spirit of rebellion, which most feel to some degree and which flared up into the independence wars of the nineteenth century. This rebel spirit is personified in a star of a different sport. To meet him we drove into northern Colombia, near the Caribbean coast, into the humid, lazy region where Colombia's Nobel Prize winner, Gabriel Garcia Marquez, set his novel *One Hundred Years of Solitude.*

At a police checkpoint on the road our driver made a routine offering of a bag of fruit to ease the formalities, and then we left the asphalt for a mud track which brought us bumping and sweating into what looked like the heart of Africa. Straw-roofed huts and a central open space, jungle all around, and black people — very black people — standing in the shade or moving lazily between the huts.

This was Palenque. The name means 'fortified village'. Palenque has a couple of hundred huts, no hospital, no doctor, no tarmac road, not much piped water, not much electricity, but, behind a huddle of rough huts, it does have a large concrete gymnasium. In a yard nearby, the heavy air trembled with snorts and thuds. Boxers, black boxers, hissing, steaming, murderous. Bags jolted by punches, skipping ropes slapping the dust. And in a ring surrounded by children, two small boys sparring under the eyes of the man we'd come to see — the pride of Palenque, Kid Pambelé. He was born Antonio Cervantes but somewhere on the way to winning the Light Welterweight Championship of the World he became popularly known as 'Pambelé'. And his popularity in South America was immense. When he first came home with the title he was paraded round the city of Cartegena on a fire engine; the president asked to see him and promised at least some piped water and electricity for the champion's birthplace; funds materialised to build that gymnasium now standing incongruously among the grass roofs; generals and ministers made the sticky pilgrimage to Palenque to inaugurate it. This village in the swamps of Colombia has only about three thousand people and yet Pambelé is not the only world champion it has produced. In the last ten

(Left) In Palenque, Colombia: tomorrow's star...

(Below)...and today's: former World Champion, Kid Pambelé.

years no fewer than three Palenqueros have beaten the world: Pambelé himself at Light Welter Weight; Rodrigo Valdez (The Terror) at Middleweight; Ricardo Cardona at Featherweight; a brother of Cardona came close to the World Bantamweight crown, and Pambelé's brother has also nearly reached the top. And, as those laughing children who were now watching Pambelé teach two infant sluggers to duck, weave and slam, would tell you, their village has another World Champion on the way in Heriberto Torres, a supple young fighter determined to follow in the illustrious Pambelé's footsteps.

Boxing is not an especially South American sport, but the reason why this village has become a cradle of champions is historically South American. Kid Pambelé's ancestors were brought to South America quite early in the Spanish conquest, in about 1540, as slaves, shipped from Guinea in West Africa. They were spirited people who did not take kindly to enslavement. They rebelled repeatedly and in 1599, in one of their uprisings, they fled and set up a camp in the swamps. 'Free Palenque' they called it, and the Spaniards of course soon came clanking through the jungle in their helmets and breastplates to put an end to it. But time and time again the impossible happened and the Palenqueros fought off the Spanish. And, not content with mere defence, the escaped slaves became some of South America's earliest guerillas and took the fight to the Spaniards with hit-and-run raids. The Palenqueros were masters of rebellion and by 1621 the Spanish were actually reduced to signing a peace treaty allowing them to come and go freely.

It didn't last long, of course. Eighty years later the Spanish were offering a price for black heads and sticking them on poles. In the end it was not just the fighting spirit of the Palenqueros which kept them free, but also economics. In the nineteenth century slavery was abolished, the coastal cane fields ceased to be so profitable and the land-owners moved inland and began to offer work on a less unequal footing.

The spirit of rebellion which Kid Pambelé and the Palenqueros embody seems to be dear to the South American soul. In the last twenty years hardly a country in the whole continent has been free of guerilla warfare. Pambelé is a product of that rebellious spirit as well as its symbol, and life in Palenque has been shaped by rebellion for three and a half centuries. It still is, as we would see later.

Pambelé left the sparring children and walked through the village of his childhood. His hands hung loose in the potently relaxed way that boxers sometimes have. 'I had only three years of schooling' he murmured, his eyes smiling and yet always seeming to be measuring you for a punch. 'My parents couldn't afford more. But I'm intelligent. I feel it. I learn quickly. And I've seen all four seasons of the world'. Probably he meant his travelling to fights — to the USA, Thailand, South Africa and Korea but there was no time to ask him because we'd arrived at a hut that served as the village bar, and the star was surrounded by old men patting him with one hand, drinking with the other. In the smart hotels of Cartagena, where Pambelé lived now, the barmen would start to mix a Campari and Soda as soon as the champion came in, but here in his birthplace he was drinking sweet black beer.

(Above) Pambelé and friends — sons of rebellion.

The people were friendly enough to me as the guest of their star, but I'd already seen enough of the Palenqueros to know that without him there'd have been no welcome for a white. My first encounter with any-one from the village had been on the beach in Cartagena. The village women — the Palenqueras — go there to sell fruit, and I had bought a wedge of pineapple from one — a tall muscular girl with a basket on her head. Without realising that I was being drawn into what, for her, was a routine skirmish with a white, I was starting to point out that she hadn't given me my change when she blew up in my face. Her ferocity seemed out of all proportion to the few pesos. She was suddenly a growling virago, vehement, contemptuous, even menacing. I backed off, lost for words, embarrassed, confused — an ineffectual *gringo*. She strode away haughtily, a raging pillar of black rebellion, walking towards the massive fortress walls of Cartagena which men of my race had forced her ances-tors to build. I was left feeling it had been my fault. Palenqueras one point, white men nil.

(Above) Hard woman. A
Palenquera in Cartagena.

(Below) Cradle of stars.
A typical Palenque home
and kitchen.

(Right) Kid Pambelé's
people — evening tide near
Palenque.

What I hadn't known then was that the Palenqueros' spirit of rebellion still made it desirable to score off a white man whenever possible. It was not a thing of the past in Palenque. Aggression was still fostered there, less intensely but in much the same way as it had been when the village of runaways was always ready to fight off the Spanish. In those times Palenque became a black Sparta, a warrior state. Aggression was inculcated in all Palenqueros. Everyone had to learn to fight, boy or girl, man or woman; the people were divided into combat groups rather as soldiers are divided into platoons.

And they still are. To see how aggression is nurtured in Palenque we had to go to the village water hole. Surprisingly there was no question of Pambelé's going with us. Though he was a product of the training, the rituals of the water hole were the province of women and children only. It would be possible for me to see only because I had been brought to the village by an anthropologist, Nina de Friedman. Nina had earned an acceptance rare for whites. In the course of studying the Palenqueros and writing about their ways she had been allowed to live amongst them for months on end. But even she was nervous of approaching the water hole. She led us beyond the huts at the low end of the village and down a bank of glistening mud to a brown river. Cautiously she advanced to a point where we could see through the trees to a shallow bend where the river widened out in dappled sunlight. Young girls passed us carrying heavy drums of water on their heads, their backs straight as steel rods as they climbed the steep and slippery river bank behind us. In front, at the shallow bend, women stood and sat in the river washing clothes or bathing while children played around them. Some of the children were fighting, and Nina explained to us that fighting among Palenque children was not usually the spontaneous kind common to most children; here it was a ritual. A little girl would scoop out a hollow in the gravel by the river and with cupped hands lift some of the clean water from it. And another child would challenge. Formally she would demand 'Give me that water hole. It is my right'. 'No', would reply the first little girl, following a form handed down from her mother, 'This is my water. I was here first'. The tone of the voices would become lower, threatening; a straight left would flash to the challenger's ear, and the fight would be on. Encouraged by the mothers, who sometimes fought as well, the children would punch and grapple in what was an historic preparation to face the world outside — a world which had been hostile to them for four hundred years. In spirit Kid Pambelé's people are perpetual guerillas. And it is that which has made the village into a cradle of stars.

For the poor in South America there is always much to rebel against of course. Inequality and exploitation are the norm. As the sun began to go down over the swamps the descendants of men and women who had thrown off the exploiters began to bring in the cattle. One of them, an old man now, was a survivor of a massacre described by Garcia Marquez in *One Hundred Years of Solitude*: a village full of workers had struck for better pay from a multi-national fruit company and, with simple finality, they had been machine-gunned. The corpses and the evidence had been spirited away in sealed trains, and one of the few survivors of this piece of South American labour relations which had never officially happened fled home to Palenque. He brought with him a valuable piece of knowledge. In the world outside Palenque, while working for the fruit company, he had seen for the first time men boxing — for money. He brought back to Palenque the news that the fighting skills which were routine to people there could earn high rewards. And so began Palenque's emergence as the most successful academy of boxing in the world.

It was sunset, and in the village square, now that the air was cooling, they had put up a boxing ring. The star stood beside it, his hands still loose but now in big red gloves. Around him danced the village band, drumming and singing like something out of Africa, 'Pam-be-lé! Pam-be-lé! Pamm! Bay!! Lay!!' The crowd sighed happily, and their star, the man who had demonstrated to the world their invincibility, climbed up into the ring with a cautious sparring partner and loosed the first blows in a demonstration of what for the South American blacks of Palenque, relegated to the bottom by the world outside, has been an ennobling art.

What made those Palenque people so unusual was that they had rebelled and had gone on rebelling. In Brazil, in Rio, where we went to meet our third star for a final insight into the South American soul, there seemed to be poverty enough to spark a French Revolution. But no such explosion had occurred: at the top a military government had stayed in power almost unchallenged in recent years; at the bottom, in the *favelas* with their slimy water and sour smells, one generation of the poor had brought up another without any significant protest. No one had rocked the boat. There had been little sign of the Palenque spirit.

Even in the slums there are television sets and there, according to some students of the South American condition, lies part of the explanation for this lack of rebellion. A boxer may represent rebellion, a bullfighter may inspire courage, but many people don't watch them. Their influence is very limited. But nearly everyone watches television. It is the new universal literacy. We followed an audience researcher from door to door on a vast housing estate in a poor suburb of Rio. What had they been watching? Had they enjoyed it? What, we really wanted to know, was the message beamed to their souls by the most widely received medium in the land and by its stars?

What they had all been watching without exception turned out to be what the South Americans call *'Telenovelas'* and we call 'Soap Operas'. South Americans love soap operas, and many of their TV channels put out three in a row, right through peak viewing hours every night.

Many of those 'soapies' are made in Rio in one of the world's biggest television and publishing corporations, the privately owned Rede Globo organisation. In Brazil alone Globo's soap operas draw fifty-six million viewers every night. Fifty-six million! What do those people want to hear? What do they admire? What sort of character strikes a chord in their souls? Who are their stars?

Cristina Mullins has been starring for Globo for several thousand episodes of a dozen different soapies now. It has brought her fame, and a certain influence. Rushing from the studio to the canteen for a quick

FACES FROM A BLACK SPARTA.

(Left) Their ancestors came as slaves and defied their Spanish masters.

(Above) They won freedom but they're still underdogs.

(Below) The stars they admire are fighters.

Brazilian coffee, she told me, 'If I wear my hair in a particular style on the show tonight, half the women in Brazil will be copying me before the week's over'.

Proof of the power of the example set by the star was that it has commercial value. She and Globo were often paid by marketing agencies to show her using a particular brand of sauce or soap as part of a scene in the show. But, commercial influence aside, what type of example did Cristina set as a character? To her viewers was there any consistent message in the women she portrayed? How did Cristina Mullins characters behave? Cristina had no time to answer that question right there. Already we were hurrying back to the studio for her next scene. It was hard work being a TV star in Brazil. Soap operas everywhere, from Dallas to Coronation Street, are made like cars on conveyor belts, but Globo's belt ran faster than most.

Watching Cristina at work on the set, I began to understand the character she was playing. Cristina is a blond Brazilian with green eyes. Her brow is high and rather serene, her eyes are grave. There is about her something of a Madonna. And so there was in the role she was playing. She opened the door of a middle class living room full of heavy old furniture to be faced by a young man who had clearly brought bad news. From his gestures as he unfolded that news to Cristina it became clear that it was worse than bad. It was so appalling that he could hardly bring himself to tell her. Unable to understand Portuguese, I could nevertheless gauge the seriousness of the news from his face and it was a calamity of the first magnitude. At the very least the star was being told that her child had just died. I waited to see how the young woman whom Cristina was playing would react: with hysterics? With choking sobs? With anger even, at the cruelty of life? None of those. When the messenger's last tragic word had faded, Cristina moved slowly away from him: she would bear this suffering alone. Gently, conveying infinite resignation, she leaned against a window frame and stared through cloudy eyes into the distance. Everything about her spoke of patience, of tolerance, of turning the other cheek. She was a consummate madonna.

And in a single scene I had seen borne out something that analysts of South American television have contended: that whereas the models in **our** soap operas are often tough people who fight their way up with varying degrees of cunning and nastiness, the models in South American soapies set a quite different example.

Every night there are many characters like the one played by Cristina, all putting across a conviction which has been an important part of the South American soul for so long that it would be wrong to suspect those who control the television channels of calculatingly dispensing valium, of consciously trying to suppress discontent in their seething cities, of moulding their message to uphold the status quo. No one plots the message, no one manipulates. It simply reflects the way things are, and never questions the status quo: the sun rises, the sun sets; the rich are rich, the poor are poor. And, like Cristina's stricken character, those who suffer must not be angry, must not protest. They must show patience, acceptance, grace.

In the studio, the recording of the episode was over. One more story was in the can. Soon it would be beamed from transmitters which stood high above Rio behind the giant statue of Christ. The message would fall like manna onto fifty-six million people below. I went with Cristina to a meeting of directors and scriptwriters to discuss her next role. They were talking about her madonna quality and how it was going to be invoked yet again in her next role. She would face hardships, she would be beset by injustice and misfortune. But she would never become angry. She would endure, she would tolerate, she would turn the other cheek. She would express the belief planted deep in the South American soul that, though courage and rebellion may be important, patience and humility will earn their rewards in heaven and it is the meek who will, one infinitely far-off day, inherit the earth.

(Right) A star and her admirers. Cristina Mullins on her way to film episode 437 of a Brazilian soap opera.

TYRANTS
WILL RISE FROM
MY TOMB

C H A P T E R 4

There are countries in South America where it is difficult not to become paranoid, where prying eyes and straining ears seem to follow wherever you go. That is how it was in Chile in 1984. So much covert attention was paid to us that we began to feel like celebrities. So we were not as surprised as we might have been when a routine telex from me to our Executive Producer in Sydney, Peter Reid, was interrupted. In the middle of the message which I had drafted, and handed in to the telex office, there appeared during transmission a strange addition. It read: 'This is a line message from the telex operator to Mr Pizzey and Mr Reid. Can anyone call me at home (a Santiago phone number followed), not from the hotel here, at midday Chilean time? Yesterday it was impossible to say you something. If you don't do that please take care and note that I am an opposition man. Somebody from the secret Chilean police was asking for you yesterday. It was the security man who is on the twelfth floor, blonde with moustaches. Sorry, is the only way I have to give you this secret info.' ¶What to do about it? After two weeks in General Pinochet's Chile I'd seen enough to know that a message like that couldn't safely be treated as a joke: Chile was a police state.

It was a state where strangers would watch you filming in the street and then, once they had worked out that you were a foreign journalist, they would come over and whisper that they felt they could tell things to you which they wouldn't dare say to any Chilean, and that you must please tell the world what was happening in their sad country. I still have a note put into my hand by a small boy while we were filming at a country railway station. Presumably written by his invisible father or mother, it translates as 'As you are foreigners and perhaps journalists, it would give me great pleasure if you would publish the things that are happening in Chile. Today we have one of the highest rates of infant mortality, illiteracy, prostitution. The Lord Pinochet holds onto government on a basis of terror and by the exemplary deaths of priests and union leaders who oppose him. Please, if it is possible, publish this'. Everywhere there was a feeling of being watched. A comedian in a bar hurriedly drew a crowd round him and dashed off some mildly political jokes. 'We must be quick', he urged the crowd, 'while the police have gone to lunch'. In a slum outside the capital people celebrated another year of poverty with a march by their children. 'We've been here a year', the kids sang, stepping around puddles of filth, 'and this is all we have'. The telephone operators in our hotel often seemed to know about our movements and sometimes even about our plans. And what they didn't already know, they tried to discover: 'I heard you'll be going to Argentina', one voice on the line said. 'I wonder if you'd take a parcel for my sister? Oh, and when exactly are you going?'

Gloria, my wife, was followed, usually by the same obvious security man, even when she went to the hotel restaurant. Marc, the assistant cameraman, became so frustrated with the clumsy sleuth who was his appointed shadow that he walked into the hotel men's room, spun round and walked straight out again, right into the oafish man who had been waiting at the door deliberating on whether or not to follow him inside. A visiting party of British Members of Parliament and trade unionists had their hotel rooms broken into and their notes (and only their notes) stolen. A juggler in a fairground threatened that, unless we included his act in our filming, he'd report us to the secret police: he didn't say what for. After a week of this sort of thing a connection was made in Gloria's mind: 'I know where I've felt like this before', she muttered as we got out of a taxi whose driver's ears had been noticeably straining to catch our conversation, 'In Russia'.

And now the telex. I weighed it up: 'Can anyone call me at home, not from the hotel'. It seemed to me that if the man were genuine he was alarmingly clumsy. If he really wanted to help us there were far less conspicuous ways of saying so than by announcing in a telex his willingness to commit what a military court would call Treason. If he *was* genuine, he was best ignored. And if, as seemed more likely, he was not genuine but was trying to lure us into some action which could be used as a justification for expelling us, then it was still best to ignore him. With that resolved I went out into the square in front of Chile's presidential palace, La Moneda. Its pleasant colonial facade had long been replastered to fill scars from the shells with which the present occupant had displaced his

(Page 74) President Pinochet of Chile.

(Overleaf) Chilean ski troops.

predecessor. In front of the gates, once smashed by tanks, a general of the military government was being driven past a goose-stepping guard of honour, in the direction of his headquarters.

It seemed a typical image of South America — land of military dictators and coups. In fact, that image is somewhat misleading. Our picture of South America does tend to be one of a continent under the jackboot, but military dictatorship is actually on the wane at the moment. It is likely that by the time these words appear in print the number of countries in continental South America without elected governments will be only two — Chile and Paraguay. Whether this decline in military governments will prove permanent, or whether it will turn out to be just the swing of a pendulum soon to fall back again towards rule by men in uniform is impossible to say. But either way, South America's reputation as a land of dictators is not undeserved. Historically there have been many, and why that has been so was one of the things we wanted to learn about.

In Peru, on the outskirts of Lima, we went to a museum in a house which had once been the military HQ of Simon Bolivar, 'The Liberator'. In the first part of the last century Bolivar and his fellow leaders of the great movement for South American independence from Spain had done much to lay the foundations of South American politics for the next hundred and fifty years. We stood looking at a giant sculptured head of Bolivar, so big it almost filled a room. It was easy to understand the powerful impression he had made on people. His mistress, Manuela, had written to her jilted English husband, 'If I had left you for a man you would have cause to complain, but I've left you for a god — for Bolivar!' He was mercurial, inspired, visionary. He was 'The Liberator'.

Born in Venezuela when South America was still ruled by Spain and Portugal, Bolivar went to Europe to study, and there he took to heart the ideas of The Great Enlightenment. He returned to South America speaking of 'the sweet agitation of freedom' and affirming that the greatest satisfaction a people could obtain was 'The glory of living under laws dictated by their own will'. After three centuries, the rule of Spain was no longer tolerable to native-born South Americans like Bolivar. He became the greatest of the leaders of an independence movement which erupted from one end of the continent to the other. The rule of Madrid had to be ended. It would not be easy. Bolivar fought his way down South America on a tide of blood and destruction, slowly crushing the Spanish rulers, setting up one new nation here and another there, pausing just long enough to dictate an impracticable constitution, then struggling on to new victories. The campaign was a triumph but Bolivar was a realist. Before the great adventure was over he had realised that his dream of a free and united South American people was going to fail. 'He who serves the revolution here' he said' 'is ploughing the sea'.

But despite his own realistic assessment of his failure there is hardly a city in the continent which is not still being liberated by a proud statue of Bolivar. His influence was enormous: you will find him still celebrated in bronze in Argentina, in Chile, in Bolivia, in Peru, in Ecuador, in Colombia, in Venezuela, and even far away in Brazil. It is like finding statues

of the same man in every nation of Europe, except that in Europe there really is no one statesman who has ever inspired such widespread and visible homage.

How was it that a man whose achievements still command such respect failed to establish the democratic rule which he wanted for all South Americans? If you look at the statues of Bolivar you will see that he is wearing uniform, and that is part of the problem. In order to become a liberator and break the hold of imperial Spain he had to become a general. And once his forces had succeeded in driving out the Spanish, the general faced a crisis which made it difficult to put his uniform aside and become a genuinely civilian leader: in his newly liberated domain administration was suddenly impossible, the bureaucracy was collapsing. For three centuries everything had been organised by experienced Spanish administrators, with decisions documented, copies going to Madrid, and royal instructions coming back. But now that Bolivar had banished Spain there was a vacuum.

He himself had said that no form of government was as vulnerable as democracy so it followed that its institutions needed to be strong. But with Spanish rule gone there was a profound weakness in the bureaucracy, in the judiciary, in the executive. And chaos threatened from many quarters: in the wake of the independence wars regional conflicts and class rivalries were boiling, the cities were in ruins, the farms were neglected, the economy was devastated. Firm action was needed to avert catastrophe, but the apparatus of government was enfeebled. There was only one institution which was strong — the new and victorious military. And so, perhaps inevitably, Bolivar filled the power vacuum with the strongest **organisation** to be found — the army. And the leadership fell to the strongest **men** to be found — himself and his fellow commanders.

So it was that the 'Liberator' became modern South America's first dictator. By most accounts Bolivar fulfilled his omnipotent position with justice and wisdom, but he knew that despite his democratic leanings, he was laying the foundations of a series of dictatorships; and, perhaps worse, he also knew that lesser men would succeed him. Despairingly the Liberator said 'Tyrants will rise from my tomb'.

And they did. For six generations since Bolivar's time dictatorship — and too often tryanny — has been common in South America. The irony of this is emphasised in a piece of film from 1930: it shows a statue of the Liberator being unveiled by the then ruler of Venezuela — Juan Vincente Gomez. Gomez is a classic dictator — one of those tyrants prophesied by Bolivar — and there, in the very country of the Liberator's birth and on the anniversary of his death, was the dictator Gomez paying homage to Bolivar who would have detested him.

Gomez was typical of the rulers who have given South America its reputation for dictatorship. He was a *caudillo* — a strongman — as such rulers are known. Almost uneducated, he had a wily flair for power. Men feared and followed him, the Venezuelan Indians believed he could read their minds, and by the time he was unveiling that statue to a long dead Bolivar, Gomez had already held Venezuela under his thumb for a quarter of a century. Gomez knew well why the nation submitted to him:

(Above) The Chilean
Junta — Pinochet 2nd
from right.

'The people need dictators', he explained. 'They are a primitive race living in a backward country. A despot represents their unconscious desire for order. Without order they feel lost.'

And 'order' he gave them. But not much else. Under the rule of Gomez, Venezuela became rich; it was the second biggest exporter of oil in the world. But the living standard of the mass of people remained miserable. As has often (but not always) happened with dictators, much of the money went on the police, on the army and on those close to Gomez. Education, feeding the poor, justice — those things which men of Bolivar's stamp would have identified as the foundations of human growth — were not priorities for Gomez. 'Keep the army happy and the people down' was the creed of dictators.

When Juan Vincente Gomez finally let go of life and of power in 1935, there was rejoicing. But after him came more military governments. So Venezuela, like many other nations of South America, remained what a disgusted Bolivar had said it was over a hundred years earlier — 'a barracks'.

But why has dictatorship flourished for so long in South America? Bolivar's failure explains something of how it took root, but nothing of why it has been able to go on blooming for six generations — nothing of why dictatorship lived on to become a dominant theme of South American history.

FOR DEFENCE OR TYRANNY?

(Left and right) The armed forces of Chile and (above) Bolivia.

To seek part of the answer to that we travelled to Bolivia. If the travelling were as easy as writing that sentence, then answers would be far more accessible in South America than they actually are. But part of the fascination of the place is its cussedness. Travel is often so difficult that the seeker of answers forgets all about his quest and has to concentrate on just getting to the next stop. In the Bolivian town of Cochabamba we'd attended a garden party for the local political elite, and now I needed a taxi. I needed it for a three-day journey, and it was that need which brought into my life a man who came to be known respectfully as 'Don' José.

Around the main square of Cochabamba, beneath sunlit palms and a stone condor alighting on a Greek column, I searched for a taxi. I wanted one willing to take me across the Andes to the mining centre of Oruro where the film team had gone ahead. 'To Oruro?' I said brightly, laying before men gently polishing old taxis what I thought must be an attractive opportunity. 'And maybe then on to Siglo Veinte and down to La Paz?' But there was no enthusiasm. Evidently the prospect of three days' driving and many rugged kilometres did not appeal: these were city drivers, content with gentle trips between the hotel and the station, the bank and the town hall. But one man was different. He was taller and greyer and older than the rest, and rather stooping. But he found the prospect of a break from routine immediately attractive. We agreed on terms and drove off to his home to prepare for the trip. Old José's preparations were quite thorough. In the driveway beside his pleasant suburban villa his two sons changed the oil, put on a roof rack for my case and for a box of film lamps which I was carrying. Into the back seat they put an extra spare wheel. Then with the car prepared for the trip, they

(Below) Cyclist negotiating train lines on the road to Oruro. We were less successful. Altiplano, Bolivia.

turned their attention to their father. Swiftly José was fitted with a big peaked cap and driving gloves and a warm-looking poncho was spread on his back seat. All this took an hour, and by the time the old man and his worn Datsun were ready, it was late afternoon. It needed another half hour to queue for petrol — a strike had made it scarce — and then we were off, heading towards the mountains. As he drove, José's long body curved forwards to keep his face close to the top of the windscreen; his head tilted back so that his profile fitted the rake of the screen, and he peered down his long nose at the road. He gave off waves of enthusiasm and a smell of an old man. There was about him an elegance and a touch of chivalry. Rather than a taxi driver he could have been an eccentric millionaire, I thought, as we began to climb up from the plain through villages striped with shade in the evening sun. Then we were moving higher, into the balding hills. The air became noticeably thinner; we passed a wrecked bus with one side still brightly painted but the other ripped away from nose to tail. As the bus ran out of control it must have been ground against the rocky mountainside and rubbed away like cheese against a grater. Even the seats on that side had been ground away. José and I muttered to each other about the fate of the passengers and hauled slowly past the wreck, and on up towards the darkening sky. So far the road had been smooth and modern, but by the time night fell, the two lanes of asphalt had given way to just one of rocks. The road had become a mountain track.

Only one of José's headlamps was working. We'd climbed very high by now, but in the lamp's weaving beam the track ahead still wound upwards around the shoulders of the mountains. It was innocent of all road signs, crash barriers and fences. I glanced beside me at José. He was still craned forward, chin out, neck stretched and profile aligned with the windscreen, peering down through old spectacles. I wondered how much he could see. What I could see was beginning to frighten me. As we approached each new bend the crumbling edge of the track would suddenly appear across our path instead of beside us where it had been a moment before. That was how the bends announced themselves; at those moments our single lamp beam would pick out the rocky edge before disappearing into the black void beyond. Often José's reaction to these sudden nothingnesses was slow, and he would spin the wheel at the last second: the car's nose would finally swing sideways across the blackness so late that it obscured the edge of the bend which by then was right under our front wheels. This went on for bend after bend, and I — sitting on the outside edge — grew tenser and tenser: I would jam my feet down on the imaginary brakes, my stomach would rush up to the back of my throat and I'd gulp down the cold air. Beside me old José was farting strongly.

Hours later we were over the Andes. We were bowling along the flat *Altiplano* towards Oruro when we were caught by that same Bolivian indifference to safety which had left the steep tracks behind us unfenced. Without any warning sign a railway line crossed our path: José didn't see it at all and I caught only a glimpse of the shining rails sticking up from the road before we were airborne. José was no pilot and he made a poor

SHACKS AND PALACES.

(Left) A Santiago suburb.

(Below left) Tent city put up by Santiago's homeless.

(Right) La Moneda — the President's Palace.

(Below) Santiago's business quarter.

(Right) A future president?
Officer cadet in Valparaiso
Chile.

landing, skidding wildly to one side then over-correcting to the other, veering wider and wider till it was obvious we were going to go off the road again. I huddled down with arms over face; old José, still composed at the wheel, farted with exertion, the car made one final drastic skid and then we took off again over the edge of the embankment and into darkness. Surprisingly we didn't roll, but landed upright on the plain below. With a final swivelling skid, we crunched to a stricken stop. The roof rack had sheared off throwing luggage and film lamps across the desert gravel. José was shaking and muttering in the icy night air.

But the old gentleman recovered well over a brandy and we finally reached Oruro. Quickly he regained enough of his style to win the respect of the other drivers who had been waiting for us. Soon they had given him the honour of a 'Don' before his name and it was clear that Don José was now a member of our team. So be it. I resolved that whenever we were driving at night in future we would put another car in front of Don José's as a pathfinder. Then I turned my thoughts back towards dictatorship and the question of what factors had enabled it to flourish so long and so often in South America.

It was some days before we found a new clue to that. And the clue appeared in an unlikely setting. We had stopped for petrol on a journey through the hills. Because of another Bolivian strike, we were facing a long queue in a place which was just a handful of huts. The nearest thing to a transport cafe was a low mud house with a bench outside and a row of big earthenware pots. In each pot was brewing cloudy maize beer — chicha. The hospitality of the local Indians was generous and they were soon ladling out far more samples than we fancied of the different brews, each with its head of scum and insects. Through an increasing haze I noticed a wall-chart above the pots and, asking to see it, found that I had hit on both the clue I was looking for and a burning local issue.

The wall-chart showed the presidents of Bolivia. They looked down on the bar from rows of stamp-sized portraits. The recent presidents wore modern suits or army uniforms, the early ones wore the dark blues and reds of the period a century and a half ago when Bolivia had been founded as a nation and named after Bolivar.

In the one hundred and fifty years since then the nation had had one hundred and eighty-six presidents. One hundred and eighty-six! 'Useless! All of them!' was the verdict of the chicha- drinkers, 'All they want is to stuff their pockets!' The locals pointed their glasses at the crowded gallery of national leaders, 'No good! No good! They're a shame on our nation.' For those disenchanted locals the chief concern was naturally the greed of their swiftly changing governors and its effect on their own pockets. But for us, in our search for reasons, what seemed more significant was that swiftness itself: one hundred and eighty-six presidents in one hundred and fifty years reveals gross instability. And, though no other country in South America has a record quite as frenetic as Bolivia's, political instability has been widespread. And when governments keep falling, chaos threatens. And then the stage is set for the strongman — the dictator — to take over. Backed by the army he appears as the only leader who can restore order.

(Left) Viva the Generals?
Political rally in Bolivia.

(Above) A decade without
the vote. Chilean farmer.

(Right) Chilean winter.

91

But why such instability? What has made government such an insecure business in South America? The answer to that began to emerge when we reached one of the great tin mines of Bolivia. *Siglo Veinte* it was called — 'Twentieth Century' — but its story was the story of four centuries in South America. Bolivia's *Siglo Veinte* mine has been a great source of wealth for countries outside Bolivia and, in that, it had continued a draining off of the continent's wealth which first began when the *conquistadores* plundered South America's gold and silver. They took away riches sufficient to transform the economy of what was then the developed world — Europe. Ever since then South America has been seen as the land of Eldorado, a jackpot of a place, full of wealth for the taking. And its wealth has been taken on a scale which has left its own nations economically weak and unstable. Of course some South Americans have grown rich in the process. Simon Patiño, the poor Bolivian miner who started the *Siglo Veinte* mine, became one of the richest men the modern world has seen.

Simon Patiño had palaces in Europe, mines abroad as well as at home, and fine houses in Bolivia even though he was seldom there in later life. Patiño himself did well, but his country's share of the profits for its tin mines has not been all it might have been. Tin is by far the richest asset of Bolivia, and it is estimated that if all the money made from tin had been invested at home, then Bolivia could now be among the more prosperous countries of the world. But the tin profits were not invested at home, and now, far from leading the world in industry, Bolivia leads it only in child mortality: the death rate of Bolivian children under five is forty per cent — a figure matched by only one other country in the world, Haiti.

The fact that first Spain, then Britain, then the United States had exploited South America (and the fact that many South Americans had helped them do so) went some way to explaining why the economies of many South American countries were weak. But weakness alone did not explain why they were politically unstable — why they fluctuated so drastically as to produce the chaos which opened the way for military takeovers. After all, a weak economy did not necessarily have to be unstable; it could simply be poor but constant.

The answer to that lay in Bolivia too. We looked at one of the palatial homes of Patiño, that Bolivian who had founded the *Siglo Veinte* mine: a sumptuously inlaid billiard table glowed in a room of pillars and mosaics; a grand piano waited in the richly panelled concert hall; marble terraces stretched away into gardens on a grand scale. They were the rewards of a man who had succeeded for a time in doing something which few South American countries had ever achieved: Simon Patiño had managed to control the world price of the produce which made him rich. He had done it by buying not only Bolivia's mines but also their principal competitors in Malaya — a coup which made sure that his own personal economy would be unassailable. But that is not the story of *national* economies in South America. South Americans have not succeeded in grabbing the strings which control world prices for their exports and that is why their economies have been so unstable. Bolivia's is almost a one-product economy: it depends heavily on tin exports. And that dependence on one product whose price is fixed elsewhere is a common story in South America.

We found it again in Chile. In the desert behind the old port of Iquique, amid rusting machinery and derelict factory buildings, was a house which spoke as eloquently of failure as Patiño's palace had of success. The house had been built for the manager of what was once a nitrate plant. Until the 1920s nitrates had been the pillar of Chile's economy — sixty seven per cent of the national income in fact. We walked through the empty old house, stepping round holes in the floor, ducking under sagging lintels. The manager's house told the typical South American story: typically its occupant had been foreign — an Englishman working for an English company which had grown rich on Chile's nitrate; typically the world price of nitrate had been controlled outside Chile and had eventually crashed; and typically the effect on the nation's economy had been disastrous. Untypically Chile had recovered eventually by finding a new resource to depend on — copper; but typically the world price for that was beyond Chile's control, and a decision by the United States to cut copper imports from Chile was now rocking the nation's economy. Ironically Chile was being forced to celebrate its Day of National Independence by devaluing the peso by twenty-five per cent!

Our search for the reasons why South America had been so prone to dictatorship was bringing us to conclusions: one cause of economic instability lay in dependence on too few exports whose prices depended on outside forces; from that instability sprang the repeated threat of chaos which often ushered in the military.

And why the military? Why were generals seen as the saviours of South American nations in chaos? Well, they had played that role ever since Bolivar had given it to them. And, unlike us, South Americans had become accustomed to being ruled by men in uniform. From the abandoned nitrate plant, we travelled back across the desert to Iquique and watched Chilean troops drilling in the garrison there. That garrison had once been commanded by the soldier who was now ruling the country, Augusto Pinochet. And it was in this region that, as a young officer, he had first been ordered into political rather than purely military action. The story of Pinochet's first armed foray into politics helps to show how, in South America, armies have been used and accepted in politics as a matter of routine. It also shows how democracy might not mean quite the same thing to South Americans as to us. In 1947, even though Chile had what was regarded as a fully democratic government, communists could be rounded up and put into remote places in a kind of internal exile. It was a well established form of repression which went on being used against political dissenters even during the Allende period, and it was responsible for giving the young Pinochet his start in politics. In 1947, under orders, he took part in a round-up of communists, and was then put in charge of five hundred of them interned in a derelict village beside the desert. As a young army officer he was, in fact, encouraged to see himself as a force in politics. There was nothing unusual in that. Chile's

(Above) No wealth now.
Derelict mining town,
Northern Chile.

(Left) Nitrate plains.

(Below right) Mining
millionaire's mansion.
Patiño's house,
Cochabamba, Bolivia.

(Below left) English mine
manager's derelict house,
Chile, and (below facing
page), his one time nitrate
plant .

(Above facing page)
Road to exile, across
Chile's northern desert.

history includes many instances of the army's being used to support the political status quo — to maintain the supremacy of a ruling oligarchy of landowners, bankers and foreign interests. Once, exceptionally, the army tried to challenge this system with a series of reforms. That was in the 1920s. But the move failed, and the army reverted to its customary role as the tool of the oligarchy. Everyone in South America was accustomed (enthusiastically or otherwise) to the idea that the military were in politics. Every officer cadet knows that he might one day become President. That is how it has been ever since Bolivar.

So in 1973 when, twenty-five years after Pinochet's introduction to politics, a civilian government ran into such an acute economic crisis that Chileans feared for the dwindling food supplies, there was (from a South American viewpoint) nothing very remarkable in the fact that the armed forces took over and established a military dictatorship. Indeed they had substantial popular support in their coup.

Now, eleven years later, in Santiago, we were watching the armed forces parading before the soldier who'd taken power in that coup — President Pinochet. Not everything about his rise to dictatorship had been typical: Chile had enjoyed many years without any military coups; it was regarded as South America's most democratic country; and the government he had overthrown had been one from the far left — a relative rarity in South America. But typically the elected government had been brought down not so much by politics and ideology as by economics; typically it was wild economic instability which had sparked the crisis which had produced the typical South American response — one of those leaders foreseen by Simon Bolivar when he uttered his despairing words 'Tyrants will rise from my tomb!'

(Right) Chile's Cadet of the Year waiting to salute a fellow member of his regiment — President Pinochet.

HEAVEN, HELL AND ELDORADO

CHAPTER 5

Something like two-fifths of South America is jungle. A great green hell or heaven, depending on your point of view, spreads from the vast rivers Amazon and Orinoco and their thousands of tributaries outwards into nine countries: Brazil, Venezuela, the three Guyanas, Colombia, Ecuador, Peru and Bolivia. The endless sweaty, primeval, mosquito-ridden, livid, magnificent, stultifying jungle is so vast that no one seriously trying to cover South America could afford to ignore it. And so it was that we set off from the heights of the Ecuadorian Andes down into what Ecuadorians call their *Oriente* (their 'East') which is to say their end of the Amazon basin. ¶ Jungles have never been my favourite places, and our beginning was not auspicious. Already in the past few days, Marc — despite his black belt capabilities — had been robbed in the street, we'd three times been pelted with vegetables, we'd had four punctures on the descent from the Andes, in the foothills we'd been forced to jump for our lives from a shuddering wooden house as an earth tremor struck and then our brakes had failed. I wondered if the mishaps were manifestations of my lack of enthusiasm for our visit to The Green Hell, as I imagined the jungle. Were all these punctures and misfortunes like the glass-smashings and chair-topplings of those poltergeists which some say are summoned unconsciously.

Whatever they were, it seemed unlikely they would save me from the Amazon jungles: as we drove with our brakes perilously repaired down the last slopes, my nightmare was already close at hand. We could already see the great green carpet spread out below. Pricked by the occasional glint of a river, the green stretched as far as the eye could see, and further, much further. From where we were we knew that the jungle reached for two thousand miles to the Atlantic shores of Brazil.

But that vivid green eternity below us was undeniably a magnificent sight. You couldn't help responding to it. But gnawing inside me was still that reluctance to plunge in. And I knew why. My notion of the Amazon jungle had been tinged with dread by a book. As a boy I had read the tale of Colonel Fawcett's lost expedition: its story of piranha fish stripping a man to his bones in a few scarlet seconds had impressed me. Was that what lay in those rivers now glinting below us? But there had been a worse story in the book, and it was that which had introduced me to a horror appalling enough still to occupy a place marked 'DREAD' in the filing cabinet of my imagination: it was the story of a great Amazon spider and its victims. Black and enormous, it had lowered itself from the thatch of a rest house to gorge on sleeping guests below, leaving them bloated and dead from its venom. In the Fawcett book this jungle nightmare was illustrated with a drawing explicit enough to ensure that it would live on in my mind and be waiting to meet me if I ever strayed into the Amazon.

And, perhaps because I expected it to be waiting, it was. Soon after we arrived I was standing naked at the shaving mirror one bright Amazon morning when a movement caught the corner of my eye. I took my razor from my face and glanced down. Beside my bare foot on the white tiled floor was something that looked like a clenched fist in a mink glove. Slowly the furry fingers unclenched and the creature began an hideous crawl. I was hypnotised. The spider was the size of a tea plate and its image was transmitted through my nervous system from end to end of my being, like the letters through a stick of rock candy. Mercifully it crawled away from me and disappeared unhurriedly down a hole under the bathroom doorpost.

Hopping past that dreaded hole, I pulled on my boots, remembering to check them first for scorpions. Then I broke a coat-hanger to give me a straight rod and went on the attack.

A strange figure, with shaving cream at one end, boots at the other and naked in between, I probed the hole with my coat-hanger-sword. I gave a series of vigorous lunges but felt no reassuring squelch: The brute had gone out of range. But supposing it returned? To forestall that I tore up most of a roll of paper and packed it tightly into the hole.

As I continued to shave I thought about my unwelcome guest. Or was it my host? Had it been in the room before I moved in? Reason told me that my terror was probably not rational — probably the spider was not venomous. So, even though I might never bring myself to feel warmly towards it, there was nothing really to be feared. But that idea died later when I mentioned the spider to the hotel receptionist. As I described the hairy monster, with a detachment which I think the intrepid Colonel

(Page 98) Yaminahua girl and pet. Peruvian Amazon.

(Overleaf left) Twilight on the Amazon.

(Overleaf right) The great river's headwaters. Ecuador.

Fawcett would have respected, the receptionist's eyes opened wide and he pursed his lips like a doctor diagnosing cancer. 'They're not good', he muttered, 'Not good. If she bites your finger then your arm will be swollen for a week. Even if she only crawls over you, her hairs will give you a nasty rash'.

That night I checked the hole before going to bed, and was relieved to find that what I had begun to think of as the spider's tomb, was still firmly plugged with paper. I slept well. And then woke to find that the paper had been pushed aside. Far from being entombed, my nightmare had been at large in the bedroom. In the dark! Oh Fawcett!!

That the spider had had strength enough to unseal its tomb was something I didn't want to believe. That the muscular monster had been free to crawl around the room while I slept was even worse. I took up my piece of coat-hanger and a lot of newspaper, and this time I packed the hole till it felt tight as stone. Yet the next morning it had been unplugged again. Shaving once again in my boots among the crumpled ruins of my attempt to contain the spider, I came to a decision. I don't know what the steely Colonel Fawcett would have done, but I took the coward's course — I changed to another room.

That spider confirmed for me what I had long suspected: that the jungle is hell. And there have been many men led to the same conclusion by experiences far worse than mine: dysentry, malaria, typhoid, plague, poisoned arrows. But besides realists like us, there have always been men of a more romantic view: men like Columbus who tasted the waters of one of the great jungle rivers and, finding them sweet, concluded that the river must flow from paradise and that whoever was living near its source must be the citizens of heaven; and Walter Raleigh who travelled up river also believing he would find some kind of heaven. Even today we still like to imagine that there is among the jungle Indians an innocence which we have lost. But the first white man to explore the Amazon was not looking for heaven, nor was he too concerned about hell. What lured the the *conquistador* Francisco Orellana was Eldorado. He believed that the jungle contained great riches. Everyone believed that somewhere in South America there existed a golden city ruled by a golden king, 'El Dorado' — The Golden One: the *conquistador* decided that it must lie in the jungle. It was Orellana who began the whole process of invasion of the Amazon. The moment when he headed down the Ecuadorian Andes into the green, as we had recently done, was to signal the end of some twenty-two thousand years of the forest and its people living undisturbed by outsiders. Orellana, in 1541, broke into the Amazon's ancient peace to float down the great river looking for a golden mirage. Eldorado was always just round the next bend — an attitude which has coloured developments in South America ever since. That first invader of the Amazon brought with him the seeds of change which later generations of invaders would multiply. He carried the diseases which would eventually wipe out whole tribes of Indians who had no immunity; he brought the urge to amass possessions, wealth, capital on a scale which was probably unknown in the jungle peoples and he brought the superior technology which put those people at his mercy.

(Above) Missionary plane
at Yaminahuas' village.
Peru.

But the *conquistadores* — despite all their steel and gunpowder, despite their colds and influenza, and despite their lust for gold — did not make great changes in the Amazon. They went for gold, but found only sweat and flies. There was nothing to keep them there. They enslaved a few Indians as porters, unwittingly infected others, and went away. It was the men who came after them who really began to change life in the jungle; men who came not for riches but for souls — missionaries.

Missionaries began to work in the Amazon soon after Orellana and his explorers left, and they are still coming. In a light plane we flew across the green carpet to an Indian village called Paititi in the Peruvian Amazon. Bumping along the small airstrip the plane came to a halt in a crowd of Indians — the Yaminahuas. Some wore beads looped from above the ears to the nostrils, some wore feathers in their hair, others wore jeans. The missionary wore a crisp cotton dress that would not have looked out of place at a Miami tea party. Norma Faust had lived with the Yaminahua for seven years. It had been only twenty-one years ago that the Yaminahua had first been seen by white people, isolated as the Indians were by a journey of three weeks walking and canoeing to the nearest white settlement. With the coming of the white men the Yaminahua had learned that they had been living for centuries in somewhere called Peru. And later when the missionaries arrived they learned that this Peru of which their village was a part was itself part of a universe presided over by a god.

Norma took us first to the village school. A maths lesson had the children clapping and singing out numbers. The missionary explained to us that originally the Yaminahua had used only three numbers: 'one', 'two' and 'many'. But now they needed our system of counting as a tool to help deal with our world. They'd lived by hunting and fishing before our coming, sharing the catch amongst all their village. It sounded like a Garden-of-Eden existence, though I realised I was probably being romantic in thinking so. But it did seem sad that now they needed money. They wanted to buy shirts, pots and machetes, and that had turned them into workers. The men earned now, by felling trees: not one, not two but 'many'.

Lunch in the hut where Norma had lived for seven years with no more than occasional visitors from the mission headquarters, was a treat in honour of our visit — roast monkey. Chewing the hard meat in the company of that self-contained grey-haired lady in the tea party dress, you could not but be impressed by the dedication of the missionary. Her word for the Amazon forest which hemmed us in a thousand miles deep in every direction was 'the woods'. She was clearly indomitable.

So too were Lambert and Doris Anderson at the missionaries' base, two hours' flight away in Pucallpa. They had come to the jungle thirty years before to live amongst a then recently discovered people called the Ticuna. Lam and Doris had spent their whole working lives among the Indians; their daughter Betsy had spoken Ticuna before English, which was fine with her parents because their aim in life had been to master the Ticuna language so thoroughly that they could then devise a way of writing it down. From there they had taught the Indians to read and had set about translating the Bible into Ticuna. Again I was struck by the dedication of the missionaries — Lam from Wisconsin and Doris from Pittsburg; and again the question rose in my mind, But is it good for the Indians? Couldn't they simply have been left as they were? Does everything in the Amazon have to be changed from the way it was for twenty-two thousand years? Couldn't the jungle people have been left alone?

'No, they could not', said the missionaries. 'Everything does have to change. No one can stop progress coming into the Amazon, it's impossible. And we're helping the Indians to face the changes'. Lam pointed to a Ticuna girl, Quelina. She was helping with the finishing touches to the Ticuna Bible which had been his life's work. He explained how the education and training which the missionaries had helped to give her father had enabled the Indian to win an influential place in the government of their part of Peru. Faced with inevitable invasion by a technologically superior race, the Indians had been helped by the missionaries to survive and to adopt an approach of 'if you can't beat them, join them'.

If, as Columbus and Raleigh imagined, the jungle had been a heaven for its Indians, then the coming of outsiders with their diseases and development projects threatened to turn it into a hell. And the education provided by the missionaries (together with the religion, which could be worth everything or nothing depending on your beliefs) was certainly helping the Indians to cope with the arrival of hell. But, visiting another village where missionaries had been long established, my mis-

*(Top) Carefully balanced
on the trip downriver.*

*(Left) Still carefully
balanced.*

*(Above) The last tree in
the jungle?*

*(Above right) Amazon
flood.*

*(Below right) Amazon port
— Manaus, Brazil.*

givings returned. The Indians there were the Shipibo — sturdy people with great humour and a skill in weaving and potting which is beginning to make their work known in craft shops as far away as Paris. When we looked at their village, one thing seemed strange. Among such lively and spontaneous people, it seemed odd that the houses were set in rigidly straight lines. It gave the place the look of an army camp rather than a village. I asked about this un-Indian-seeming tidiness. Had the Shipibo always arranged things in that way? No, came the answer, for most of its twelve hundred years the village had been laid out casually. It was the missionaries who had insisted on those tidy-minded, oh-so-proper straight lines.

The missionaries' approach to the Indian is and always has been paternalistic. But at least those evangelical men and women who came to the jungle because, to them, Eldorado lay in the unconverted souls of the Indians, came with a protective attitude. But in the case of the men who came later for money, it was a different story. The first serious impact of that type of Eldorado-seeker began only about a hundred years ago. To form an idea of what it had meant we travelled down into Brazil to the city which stands in the centre of South America's jungle — a port one thousand miles from the sea — Manaus.

(Below) Indians near Iquitos, Peru.

From the babbling fish market at the docks we walked up into a city whose old houses spoke of past wealth. Few were in good repair now, but many had been built on a grand scale. What had created the wealth of Manaus a hundred years ago had been the Amazon's first experience of capitalism. In England a Doctor Dunlop invented the pneumatic tyre; rubber trees grew in the Amazon; and so began the Amazon's first great boom. For the Indians it proved to be the beginning of the end, but for the city of Manaus, it was the beginning of a bonanza. Within twenty years rubber had turned Manaus into 'The Paris of the Tropics'. It was one of the world's richest cities. At parties, dancing girls bathed in fountains of wine; there were buckets of champagne — for the horses; ladies sent their laundry home to Lisbon. One of the rubber barons had a batallion of guards, a fleet of twenty-three armed ships and a jungle territory the size of France. All of it was paid for by what the Indians called 'The Tree That Weeps' — the rubber tree.

One of the few buildings to retain its glory from those booming times was Manaus's famous opera house — the jewel of the Amazon. Walking now through the chandeliers and inlaid woods of its reception hall, I saw it as a monument to the vitality of those invaders of the jungle who had built it. But you could also see this jewel of the Amazon as a memorial; a memorial to the Indians who had died tapping rubber to provide the wealth of Manaus. On the wall of the reception hall was a painting of an Indian chief. It came from an opera which portrayed the Indians as noble and heroic, respected and even loved by the white man. But the truth had been far from that romantic fiction. It had been a truth dictated by simple economics: rubber was in demand; who knew the jungles? Who could get it out? Who could be made to do it cheaply? The Indians. How? By virtual slavery.

So the opera house was not only a gem of white enterprise, it was also an emblem of that enterprise's consequences for the Indian. Depending on your point of view it signified either pride or shame. The opulence of the splendid little auditorium was a delight: the painted ceiling from Paris, the chandeliers from Venice, the wrought iron work from Britain, the gilt pillars and red plush seats — everything was the best that the vast rubber profits could buy. But in the first ten years of this century, and in one district alone, thirty thousand Indians have died collecting rubber. Another forty thousand had been killed either for sport or for their land. One rubber baron — a man called Arana — liked to coat Indians with rubber and set fire to them. His overseer had made Indian women play blindman's bluff and shot them when they stumbled. It is estimated that, in the four centuries since white invaders first entered the Amazon region, Brazil's population of Indians has fallen by ninety-six per cent — from six million to a couple of hundred thousand today. In this present century ninety tribes have been wiped out altogether, and a further twenty-four are now close to the end. So if you took Manaus's opera house not as a gem of white enterprise but instead as a symbol of white exploitation you could gaze along its row upon row of red plush seats and say that every one of those chairs had cost the lives of fifteen thousand Indians.

PEOPLE OF THE JUNGLES

*(Above and below left)
Peruvian Indians recently
reached by missionaries.*

*(Top) Colorado Indians in
Ecuador — among the last
of a dying tribe.*

*(Top right and above)
Putting on a show for the
tourists — jungle camp near
Iquitos, Peru.*

*(Right) African blood
— in the Brazilian jungle
since slave times.*

There were also flesh and blood symbols of what our coming had meant to the jungle Indians. Near the tourist hotels of Iquitos and also across the Andes in Ecuador's coastal jungle we saw Indians who had been reduced to living as exhibits. For a fee or a gift of food they would stand while visitors stared and took photographs. It was not, you felt, what God had created Indians for. The most pathetic case was in Ecuador where a family of three who are among the very last of the Colorado Indians to survive stood like cattle, being photographed from all angles by a party of tourists. As one of the tourists had the grace to observe, it was hard work being an Indian!

Manaus's heyday had been high but soon over. In a period of less than thirty years the place had blossomed from a rough-neck frontier town into the Paris of the Tropics and then withered into a faded has-been. The decline had come about because an Englishman had taken Manaus rubber seeds to Malaya and created accessible, cheap plantations there. Suddenly the Amazon's first great boom was over. But in that first bonanza Eldorado had been sighted, and the search for more riches in South America's jungle would continue.

We steamed out onto the river. Several miles across from us, low trees marked the far banks. They were not really what I had expected of the Amazon. Shouldn't the banks of the great river be lined with giant trees festooned with lianas? Well, they were not, but the significance of that fact was only to come to me later. Meanwhile, even if the Amazon's banks were disappointing, then the river itself was vast and rather beautiful. Pink dolphins arched in the sunlight and plunged back into the brown water. There was no sign of Colonel Fawcett's dread piranhas. Later there was a fine sunset, then the river turned to blackness. I stood watching the light of an occasional passing steamer far off in the Amazon night, and I remembered an Indian legend. After all that had happened since the white men came, it was not surprising that the Indians had a legend about a devil who was white. 'Jacooruna' was his name — 'Man of the Water' — and he rose out of the river at night to kill Indians. The only way to kill Jacooruna was to tear his face off, upwards from the throat. Three white tourists had been found recently, killed in that way.

Later we travelled by plane again flying away from the Manaus region. Down below us were oil men, prospectors, lumberjacks, miners — men prepared to live in the hell of the jungle in order to pursue that Eldorado which had first been sighted in Manaus. Below us in the jungle, men's dreams and schemes of wealth grew like plants in a hot-house. Henry Ford, the car magnate, had dreamed the dream of Eldorado. Even after Manaus's boom collapsed he had bought two and a half million acres of Amazon jungle and tried to turn it into a giant rubber plantation. 'Fordlandia' he called it, with a grandiosity which is typical of Amazon projects. Fordlandia had schools, a power station, hospitals, homes for thirty thousand workers, a private railway, and no success at all. Fordlandia was a huge fiasco. The jungle proved to be a counterfeit paradise: fungus ravaged Ford's rubber trees, the Indian workers' idea of heaven was to earn a week's pay and then disappear with it, and Eldorado was nowhere to be seen. Ford quit.

Later another North American magnate — Daniel Ludwig, a shipping millionaire — attempted to make the Amazon pay. In what was probably the biggest scheme ever launched by one man he bought four million jungle acres, laid two thousand six hundred miles of road and forty-five of railway, brought in thirty thousand labourers and floated in a wood pulp mill seventeen stories high from Japan. They'd stripped a quarter million acres of forest before the Amazon hit back. Ants attacked the plantation, malaria and meningitis hit the men. A billion dollars down, Ludwig sold out. For him at least, man's biggest attempt so far to find Eldorado in the Amazon was over. And, even though the Brazilians kept part of the scheme running, it was on a smaller scale and they were working in a spirit not so much of seeking Eldorado but of trying to make ends meet.

Flying over South America's jungle brought home to you its vastness. As you sat back in a jet and began to read a novel, the green carpet stretched out down below; and hours later when you finished your novel, there was still the same green carpet below, covering the land as far as the eye could see. Perhaps it was this almost incomprehensible vastness which had fostered in South Americans their conviction that, if only they could find the key, there were riches to be had from the jungle. Fierce border wars had been fought and still were fought — over tracts of jungle, because somewhere in there Eldorado must be waiting. For the Brazilians, in particular, it was like knowing there was treasure buried somewhere in their backyard.

'The Amazon is not a problem, it's a solution', they insisted. Their thirst for Eldorado was unquenchable and their current government had put twenty billion dollars into new Amazon projects. There was gold mining, there was the Transamazon Highway, there was a hydro-electric scheme, there was 'The Project of the Century' (a great iron ore mine), there was farming, and there was logging.

The Brazilians' determination to make their 'backyard' pay had produced one of the most remarkable cities of South America — Brasilia. We left the jungle behind and flew four hundred miles down to the twenty-five-year-old city. The Brazilians had built it as the spearhead of their drive to open up the interior. Before Brasilia, all the big centres of population had been on the coast; the city was built inland three-quarters of the way towards the Amazon in order to draw people away from the coast and to encourage a movement into the interior. So now Brasilia stood in the middle of nowhere, six hundred miles from anywhere. To my eyes it was not an attractive place. But though it was a desert of a city, though its streets had numbers instead of names, though people who lived there told you bravely that they did get used to it — after six or seven years, though the Brazilian president seldom stayed in his bleak Brasilia residence because he preferred his farm, though the great architect who'd perpetrated Brasilia lived not in his sterile creation but in Rio, though the layout gave little chance to pedestrians but forced everyone into cars, and though, because Brasilia had been built where it was and in a hurry, it was — as Robert Hughes once aptly said — 'A jerry-built nowhere infested with Volkswagens', and though there were

(Top) Porter near the
headwaters of the Amazon
— Ecuador.

(Centre) The Jewel of
the Amazon — the Opera
house at Manaus.

(Below and right)
The Docks at Manaus. The
main road out is still
the Amazon.

many many things to be said against the new city, it was actually a success. Architecturally it might be a disaster, but strategically it was a success. Already Brasilia was succeeding in doing what it had been intended to do: it was drawing people into the interior. Brasilia was like a pioneer leading a migration. Already there were satellite towns all around it, teeming with Brazilians drawn towards what a national slogan had called 'a land without men for men without land'. And further north, in an area which had only recently been jungle, we watched thousands more new settlers. Already they had cleared the trees to make way for roads and new villages. The new settlers were digging the ground and scouring the rivers for gold.

For the great South American jungles, such expansion can only mean that there would be more invasion, more searching for Eldorado. And there were many who foresee catastrophe. Some ecologists even argue that the jungle, be it heaven or hell, will simply have ceased to exist by the end of this century if development continues at the present rate. But others say that is 'nonsense — that only about one per cent of the tree cover has been lost, and the jungle is big enough to survive easily'.

Which is true? In a Peruvian lumber camp we stood watching a jungle tree fall. With a final buzz from the chain-saw the great trunk swung away and crashed down, leaving a hole in the forest roof. A sad sight. But standing as we were, in thick jungle and surrounded by so many trees still growing, it seemed hard to believe that the whole jungle could really be threatened with extinction.

But then I remembered those river banks I had seen as we'd travelled down the Amazon. For thousands of kilometres those banks had not been what I had expected: they were not the high walls of a great jungle with tall trees laced with vines and echoing with bird calls. Instead, as far as the eye could see from the river, there had been only bushes and small trees. And the reason for that was that the forest had been felled long before, never to grow again. If the pursuit of Eldorado had already brought about that much unmistakable change, then might not the prophets of doom turn out to be right?

KINGS FOR A DAY

CHAPTER 6

'This country is relaxing, slothful and melancholic' a Jesuit once grumbled in Brazil, 'So that all the time is spent in fiestas, in singing, and in making merry'. In Rio at *carnaval* time it was easy to see what he meant. By the pool of the venerable Copacabana Palace Hotel, the Beautiful People were relaxing slothfully, waiting for Rio to explode into the greatest fiesta in the world — *carnaval*. Tangas — the briefest of bikinis — bared bottoms in a way which would be banned in most countries; shoals of well padded men basked on sunbeds, their oiled bodies attended by chic young mulatta concubines. Ice clinked in tall *piña coladas*. Outside, Rio slid into another incomparable sunset, and at Maxim's Cafe the transvestites and the transexuals came up from the beach and took over the pavement tables. Here and there a pretty mouth or a feminine nose graced an otherwise masculine face, but most of these citizens of the paradise city were as gaudy and crude as pantomine ugly sisters. All of them seemed outrageous, uninhibited and sad. And I, sauntering along the Copacabana promenade, was moving unknowingly towards an encounter which would be typical of beautiful, wicked Rio. As I strolled beneath the palms a tall mulatta girl eased herself up beside me. She came close and breathed into my ear something about going home together. It happened so quickly that I hardly had time to register a soft skin with a scent of clove before her hands were all over me.

For a few confused and pleasant seconds I was off-guard. Then I felt one of her seemingly many hands going for my wallet. I jumped back pushing her away, and then had to grit my teeth as she tightened a caress into a sudden crushing squeeze and vanished laughing into the crowd. I was left with my eyes watering yet laughing. That girl was Rio: beautiful, inviting, treacherous, dangerous. And, as I checked that the wallet was still in place I still felt, as I had the year before, that Rio at *carnaval* time was a wonderful place to be, even if at times it did seem to be so vicious that it could have been a twin town of Sodom or Gomorrah.

A thousand writers have tried to pin down what it is that makes Rio fascinating, and Rio has just laughed. Ideas, analysis, profundity really don't interest Rio. It has been said that Rio will never produce an Einstein, and it's not likely to produce a Tolstoy because it's too busy having a good time, and that, in Rio, a pretty girl's bottom is more significant than any theory of the universe. It's a sensual chaotic city: fifteen per cent unemployment; eighty per cent inflation; one hundred per cent panache. Perhaps the only thing that really is profound in that happily hedonistic city is inequality. The rich *Cariocas* (as all Rio people style themselves) live in Copacabana apartments which no worker could afford, even if he saved all his pay for three hundred years; development is so fast that a building is out of date and due for demolition if it's been standing for more than ten years. And this whole volcano of capitalism is overlooked from the hillsides by slums of eternal squalor. And whether or not most South Americans approve, Rio is the city which many of us outsiders imagine **is** South America.

The people of Rio will tell you otherwise: they will admit that their city has the typical problems of South America but, they will claim, it untypically has answers to those problems. Rio does have a heavy racial mix, but Rio boasts about it; Rio does have the usual South American inequality between very rich and very poor but they are all, you will be told, bursting with *Carioca* self-confidence; and Rio is the only city that worships the culture of its poor. The proof, the magic which holds the whole mix together, is the event we were soon to film: *Carnaval*.

Among the natural beauties which make Rio arguably the world's most beautiful city are its hills. Everywhere the bays and the buildings are framed by steep wooded pinnacles. It was at the end of a series of road tunnels beneath those green spires that we found the hall where one of the *carnaval* groups was rehearsing. The hall looked like an arena for indoor sports. Here, you might imagine, people from the nearby slums would come for basketball. But the hall had not been built for sport, it had been put up expressly for rehearsals for the local *carnaval* club, 'Mangueira'. Many districts of Rio, especially the poor ones, have their own *carnaval* clubs. Known as Samba Schools, these clubs are admired and supported by the locals in the way that football clubs are elsewhere. The local Samba School carries the pride of the district into the annual contest which is *carnaval*.

Inside the rehearsal hall was the thunder of drums. Perhaps thirty drummers were jolting the air with the most exciting rhythm I'd ever heard. And the people of Mangueira were parading around the hall in a

(Page 118) Rio 'chic' on Copacabana beach.

writhing snake of perhaps three thousand dancers. Every jiggling sway-ing figure was brown or black: Mangueira was one of Rio's oldest Samba Schools and everyone recognized it as a pillar of the old black tradition of *carnaval*. Other schools with white backing and professional designers had begun to change the face of *carnaval* recently, winning the prizes which for years had always gone to Mangueira and the other black schools. But Mangueira would have none of the new fashion for choreo-graphers and theatre designers and top dancers being bought and sold like football stars between rival schools. If you came from the Mangueira district, then you danced for Mangueira. Mangueira stuck to its roots in the black slums — the *favelas*.

Now out of the writhing snake in the rehearsal hall came a slender girl with the brown skin and green eyes which are the glory of the black and white mix which is called Mulatta. Without ceasing to samba she told us above the drums that she was Cledilce, our guide to Mangueira, and would we please join her in the snake? We followed her into the jumping twisting crowd and began to follow her movements. The word *samba* comes from the African *semba* meaning 'belly-button' and it is meant to be danced belly to belly. Of all the world's dances the samba is, I think, the most exuberantly sexy. 'We blacks have a lot of heat' explained Cledilce, giving my hips a loosening nudge, 'and once a year the white people come to *carnaval* to get some of it!' I tried to match the fluid grace of the dancers all around us but it was impossible: Europe was meeting Africa and finding itself stiff in the joints. Generations of Anglo-Saxon inhibitions paralized my pelvis and froze my knees. Later I would be allowed to join one of the white samba schools and dance in the *carnaval* itself. With those fellow whites my angular movements would be less conspicuous, but I would never learn to samba like these blacks. And, as a white, I would never be acceptable as a member of a traditional black school like Mangueira.

The snake wound ceaselessly round the hall, keeping us gasping for breath, and above the drums a singer crooned the words of a samba. There is a mood which the Rio people call *saudade:* it means happiness tinged with sadness, and usually sambas have it:

> *My samba says*
> *And I believe*
> *No one can be happy*
> *Without pain...*

Above the singer hung satin flags of pink and green, the colours which Mangueira always wore in *carnaval* — traditional colours, probably more important to the people of this Samba School than the national flag. And *carnaval* itself was the most important event in their year. It demanded months of saving towards the costumes and expenses, months of prac-tising and of building elaborate floats, months of gossip, teamwork, excitement, anticipation and of hoping and praying for victory.

The roots of *carnaval* go back to Roman bacchanalia and to the pre-Lenten binges of the Christians. *'Carne Vale'* meant 'farewell meat' — farewell before the rigours of Lent. Since those times, *carnaval* has

(Above) Dusk at Ipanema, Rio.

(Right) One more incomparable Rio sunset.

changed and always is changing. In Rio between about 1900 and the 1920s it was a white show, based on the *carnavals* of Cologne and with characters modelled on the Italian Commedia dell'Arte — characters like the graceful harlequin and delicate Columbine. In that rather genteel period only flutes and violins were used. But the drums of Africa were coming.

The blacks had long had a *carnaval* of their own. On the plantations there used to be a day when one black was allowed to dress up as a king, *Chico Rey* he was called, and — with dignity if not with power — he would go visiting his fellow slaves. It was a brief festival of the down-trodden which served as an annual safety valve.

In 1888 slavery was abolished in Brazil and something of that King-for-a-day tradition lived on in the slums where the newly freed blacks set up house. By 1930 their festival of King Chico had swelled into what amounted to a black takeover of *carnaval*. Samba and drums drowned polkas and violins: Africa captured Rio.

Since the 'thirties Rio's *carnaval* has grown to become world famous, always with its vitality and inspiration coming from the homes of the blacks — the *favelas*. But recently a new influence has begun to change it again: beside the earthiness of Samba Schools like Mangueira have appeared those more sophisticated and refined (if 'refined' is the right word for the exuberantly vulgar explosion which *carnaval* is) creations of Schools run by whites. Even the venue has been 'gentryfied'. Instead of the rough plank stands where, to my own surprise, I had stayed up all night, captivated by the previous year's *carnaval*, this year there was a new and massive array of concrete. A vast new '*carnaval* complex' designed by Oscar Neimeyer, the same architect who had perpetrated the soulless modernity of Brasilia. It was a subject of much distress in the *favelas* that the price of seats in this new *carnaval* palace would be beyond the reach of most of Mangueira's followers. *Carnaval* was being pulled away from the *favelas* and into the hands of richer, whiter Brazilians. Cledilce and her friends in Mangueira's Samba School dreamed of winning this year and of resisting the trend, but no one believed that they could.

On the rickety tram which climbs up from the city, you could see Rio in all its levels: rich, poor, black, white. From the business quarter of the city the tram clanged upwards past grand houses set behind high walls, past neighbourhood shops selling ice cream, beans, cold meats, coffee, past middle class apartment blocks, and on up towards the mountain-top slums. Behind and far below us lay the sea and the Sugarloaf Mountain. At our elbows brown children hung precariously from the open sides of the tram, feet dangling, as we crossed a viaduct and zig-zagged stiffly up the peak. Watching them enjoying their perilous ride brought to mind a saying I'd heard — that once a man has insurance he's dead. Part of the excitement of Rio was that it was a place where people didn't 'have insurance'. They lived with nerve, with elan. Life for them wasn't safe. It never had been. But they were alive, passionately alive.

Near the top of the peak, the tram lines ended in a grove of trees. The rich houses were far below us now. We began to walk towards a confusion of crude homes high on the hillside — one of Rio's famous *favelas*.

(Above) Saints and sinners in a Rio dealer's yard.

But before we'd gone twenty paces from the train a black man stopped us. 'Look', he said, in a friendly way. 'You really don't belong here. If you don't want to get hurt, best go back'. But coming from behind us was our guide, a man himself from the *favelas*. He smoothed our path. We strolled cautiously forward into the ramshackle world of the *favela*.

The name *favela* was taken from a wild flower which grew on hill-sides. It is a Rio irony that the human *favelas* have taken root on some of the city's very finest real estate. The world's most conspicuous slums, the *favelas* hang like an avalanche of poverty above the city, threatening it, yet, at *carnaval* time, rejuvenating it. It is another irony that Rio's *favelas* are the fruits of freedom started when freed blacks, finding that plantation owners couldn't or wouldn't pay wages, drifted to the city and set up shanty towns.

Today, nearly a hundred years later, things haven't changed very much. New homes for many of the poor have been built in massive blocks outside the city, but the *favelas* remain. Most of their population is black, and though Brazil sometimes admires its blacks, and although even many non-blacks are now adopting African religions, Rio still regards its poor blacks as a threat and its *favelas* as the 'province of evil'. And if by 'evil' you mean malnutrition, meningitis, illiteracy and violence, then the description fits.

Later, down in the city again, watching Cledilce arriving for work as a secretary, smartly dressed and crisp in an air-conditioned office, it was hard to believe that she had set out that morning from a shanty in a *favela*.

*(Left, below and right)
Rio's carnaval —
outrageous, extravagant
and THE greatest show
on earth.*

She looked as well turned out as any of us, or as any of the tourists who were beginning to fill up the smart hotels now, as *carnaval* time approached. The cafes and the beaches were crowded, offices were closing. On the streets impromptu drummers were beating out the samba rhythm which would throb beneath the city's skin until the great show exploded and then faded away for another year. *Carnaval* — **the** Greatest Show on Earth. Historically it was not surprising that Rio should be the city which produced the most magnificently frivolous event in the world. The city always had been something of a child of joy.

It was the Portuguese King Joao VI who had really set Rio on its happy course. Fleeing from Napoleon, he had bolted here from Lisbon with ten thousand courtiers. Joao became fond of the city — so much so that even when Napoleon was defeated and banished from Europe, Dom Joao refused to leave his beloved Rio for another six years. He declared Brazil equal to the mother country, Portugal. It would be from Rio, not from Lisbon, that he would rule what was then the biggest colonial empire in the world. To make of the city a capital fit for such eminence Joao encouraged artists, architects and musicians to come to Rio to develop and cultivate it. Because Brazil was seen as the bride of Portugal rather than as its slave, and because of the relatively easy-going temperament of the Portuguese when it came to mixing their blood, Rio became the capital of what was probably among the most harmoniously colonised nations in history. And out of that has come the exuberant spirit of *carnaval,* and Rio's reputation as a melting pot of races.

That melting pot image had its roots in the uninhibited approach of the early Portuguese settlers. They arrived as men without women and, it is said, on seeing the naked Indian women, they quickly learned how to make love in a hammock. Of all the world's colonisers — the British, the Dutch, the French, the Spanish — it was the Portuguese who were the most ready to mix with the natives, and to mix with them openly too. It is even said that Brazilian Indians, having observed the attitudes of various potential colonisers who landed on their shores, actually **chose** the Portuguese. And, as first brown and white mixed, and later black as well, society applauded: it was a time of expansion, Brazil needed a population, and procreation was something to be encouraged. First Asia (the jungle Indians), then Europe (the Portuguese settlers), then Africa (the black slaves) all came to Brazil. That they mixed is proved by the coffee-coloured *Cariocas* of Rio today. It is a story whose romantic side is not lost on *carnaval* revellers, and the fantasy of a lover with a different skin spices the days and nights of the festival.

But none of that means that Rio is free of racial discrimination. Even the fantasy of a *carnaval* fling with someone of a different colour doesn't embrace any idea of a permanent crossing of colour barriers. As one samba about an *'enamorado do carnaval'* puts it:

> *When the carnaval is over*
> *It's the end of our love as well*
> *Next year, God willing*
> *I'll find another.*

At one of the society balls which occupy the evenings of the rich during the week before *carnaval*, it was possible to see how little of a melting pot Rio really was. True there were blacks present, but nearly all of them were there as entertainers. They were the swirling mamas with the matronly bulk and big head scarves traditional to *carnaval*, and the long legged dancing girls from the front desks of the Samba Schools. But the guests were almost exclusively white, or very pale coffee. As one of them explained to me, there was nothing in the etiquette of Rio actually to prevent a rich black man from being invited to such a gathering of top people, it was just that there weren't many rich blacks. However much the give-and-take of the *carnaval* season might lead you to thing otherwise, the lower down the scale of wealth and position a person was, the more likely it was that he was black. In reality, Rio was no melting pot.

And this *carnaval* ball, having excluded the blacks, now seemed intent on maintaining barriers even between different strata of whites. And those barriers were physical. Ordinary guests stayed at the level of the dance floor. There they samba'd in their sequins and took champagne when their (very considerable) stamina gave out. But raised above the floor by about six feet was a row of boxes. And these were expressly designed for the glorification of those who counted for more. Here stood the top people spangled and feathered, barely able to dance because they were intent on pressing to the fronts of the boxes in order to be looked upon by the crowd just below, and by the many television cameras.

The ball was a Who's Who of Rio society, with everyone in his place. Anyone attempting to change levels and move up into the boxes was resisted by security men whose muscles bulged formidably under their dinner jackets. It was only after a fairly nerve-wracking debate with one of these guardians of the pecking order (he was holding me so that my feet didn't reach the ground) that we succeeded in elevating ourselves into the boxes and reaching the man we had come to see —'The Entrepreneur' as we called him. The Entrepreneur was the host of this ball, and a leader of the growing white influence in *carnaval*. Dressed now in dazzlingly convincing gold from top to toe and beaming down at the cameras, he was here to promote himself and his products. This was 'The Champagne Ball', staged to help him promote his new brand of the wine. And the publicity generated by the ball would also help his chain of fashion boutiques. These he had already been promoting, modelling the men's range himself. He appeared in he-and-she advertisements with his house model wearing his women's range. Together they had appeared in enough magazines to make them a fixture among the Rio glitterati. The Entrepreneur's flare for publicity was considerable. Already he had raised his model to fame by giving a reception for her in New York, presenting her with a trophy made for the occasion, and declaring her 'The World's Top Model'. What New York thought about it is not recorded, but back home in Rio nobody said 'Emperor's clothes', and The Entrepreneur made much mileage from the hype. Now he was planning to turn the *carnaval* to his advantage by appearing with his model on a float. He had bought into the Samba School which was spearheading the new and sophisticated white invasion — Beija Flor.

(Right) A Rio transexual gets that carnaval feeling.

*(Left, right and below)
The favelas — Rio's hillside
slums — have been called
'the province of evil'. They
are the source of the energy
and vitality which make
carnaval what it is.*

I had watched Beija Flor win the previous year's *carnaval*, and they had put on a splendidly rich display. Now, in their cool white and blue colours and with their designer from the world of international ballet, they were favourites to win again this year. It seemed sad to me: comparing the two teams in rehearsal I had preferred Mangueira's earthy vitality to Beija Flor's smooth sophistication. Mangueira was raw sugar, but Beija Flor was only processed cheese! But the betting put Beija Flor far ahead of Cledilce's old Mangueira. If the bookies were right, *carnaval* was going to be another defeat for the traditional *favela*-orientated schools and a triumph for the smart white set — and for The Entrepreneur. He raised both golden arms high and smiled down on the crowd below; this was **his** ball. They bounced to the drums and waved up at this Caesa of Rio society.

At the Mangueira headquarters next day the drums were silent. Last minute work was being done on the pink and green floats; a black child with a scrap of duster moved among a hundred samba drums each bigger than himself, giving a final polish. These were instruments which he hoped to be allowed to play himself when he grew up. To be in the Drum Battery was a distinction. Skirting the gleaming drums, I walked with a bundle of banknotes under my shirt, up some dark stairs and into Mangueira's office. I had come to pay the 'contribution' we would make in order to be allowed to film Mangueira when they 'went down to the asphalt' next day to make their bid for victory.

Inside the office, around a boardroom table, sat the top men of Mangueira. They were grave. Cigar smoke hung in wreaths above the trophies of old *carnaval* victories. There was no mistaking the solemnity of the occasion. As I handed over the cash to the President and mumbled a few words about good fortune in tomorrow's contest, I felt like an ambassador to a lordly court. The President was a stately old man, brownish-black with a fine head of white curly hair. He received my gift with a regal nod. Through the smoke, all the eyes in the room were now upon me. I looked again at the President and the cigar smokers around the long table. I decided that what they resembled now was not so much a king and his court as a Mafia Godfather and his lieutenants. There was silence while the President counted the bank notes. He looked into my eyes and gave me the same uneasy sensation which I had had with Pambelé the boxing champion — a feeling of being measured for the kill. Then he turned away and I knew that I was dismissed. The audience was at an end. I muttered something more about good luck in the next day's contest, and left the room to sonorous murmurs of approval from those lords of the *favela*.

To achieve such status as that President's a man must have a quality which the Rio people call *jeito*. He must be a fixer, an improvisor, a gambler. Hard work is not much admired in Rio; but the knack of coming out on top is. Organising a *carnaval* team needs a lot of *jeito*. It has become a big task. Up until 1928 it was an easy business; groups of friends simply dressed up and went out dancing through the streets. But then the first Samba School — the first organised team — was set up, and by 1935 there were twenty five of them. Mangueira, Salgueiro, Imperatriz,

Portela, Mocidade... No one could beat them, everyone joined them. As competition intensified, money became more and more important. Costly silks, satins, sequins and feathers became vital to success. Much of the funding which pays for a black Samba School's headquarters and floats and costumes has always come from illicit gambling, particularly from what is called The Game of the Animals *(Jogo de Biche)*. The game is a lottery which began quite legally a century ago as a means of raising funds for the Rio Zoo. But it grew and multiplied and then went underground. By the mid-'seventies there were thirty thousand people fully employed in running the game undercover. The turnover was a million dollars a day, and The Game of the Animals was said to be the most honestly run illegal betting game in the world. One politician has said that it is the only institution in Brazil which pays honestly and promptly. When the state authorities unwisely tried to crack down on the game, the purge backfired: it was revealed that half the policemen in Rio were taking pay-offs from the game's organisers. The game survived, and with it the main source of funding for Samba Schools like Mangueira.

So, on the evening of the great day, Mangueira, funded by illegal gambling and a small contribution from ABC TV, went 'down to the asphalt'. They were nearly three thousand strong, dressed in many different styles, but all in pink and green. And from another part of the city, on the other side of the moonlit peaks below the great Christ statue, came the favourites, in white and blue, Beija Flor. The Entrepreneur and his model arrived in a limousine. Cledilce, wearing pink feathers, tight bodice and a pink and green tou-tou, travelled with the rest of Mangueira on foot and by bus. By nine in the evening every bus, tram, lorry and metro-train in Rio seemed to be bright with members of one School or another all beginning to samba, all heading for the new concrete stadium. The start time of the *carnaval* had been scheduled — as usual — for five. It began six hours late, at eleven. As usual.

It was three hours later, at two in the morning, that Beija Flor and The Entrepreneur's turn came. And by the time Mangueira got the order to launch themselves down the avenue past the grandstands, the sun was already up. Beija Flor had been magnificent: their floats had been impeccable and lavish; their blue and white thousands of dancers had moved as one with the precision of guardsmen; after a slight hitch in getting his float under a bridge, The Entrepreneur had stood suavely elegant, anticipating victory. Cledilce and Mangueira could not hope to match that polish. Before Mangueira was half an hour into its parade, Cledilce had grown so excited that her discipline was gone. She broke the ranks to dance an exuberant solo and was smacked back into line by the School's white-haired president. But the crowd was enjoying it. They'd been in their seats since the afternoon of the day before, their eyes were heavy in the early morning light, but Mangueira was beginning to rouse them. The drums pounded, three thousand shimmering dancers sang and kicked and waved, lifting the audience gradually to its feet to wave and sing back. More and more people jumped to their feet, higher-pitched drums cut in to raise the temperature again and again until the dawn was jumping with thirty thousand people on their feet, hands high

(Above, left and right)
Kings and Queens for a day,
they've waited all night
to make this exuberant
journey past the stands.

and crooning Mangueira's song. Below the stamping audience Mangueira's ranks of black mamas swirled, eyes and teeth shining beneath pink and green head scarves; dancers now sashayed freely out of the ranks to dance their raw sugar message: vitality, earthiness, laughter, exuberance. They were the people from the *favelas* and this was *their* day.

They eclipsed all who had gone before. It was another hour before they'd danced their way to the end of the grandstands, and by then such was the enthusiasm of the crowds that Mangueira's President, showing great *jeito*, decided to break all the rules and take the School right back up the avenue again and to invite the audience to climb down from the stands and join them. The sun rose higher, Cledilce wept tears of jubilation, the audience flowed down to mix with the pink and green, the drums whacked out a victorious crescendo. There was no doubt: the old vitality of the *favela* had triumphed over the sophistication of the smart set. Raw sugar had beaten processed cheese. It was the hour of Mangueira. They were kings-for-a-day. At the end of the avenue the crowd, now bearing the three thousand pink and green dancers along, began to melt away towards buses, taxis, lunch. Soon the kings would be back in the *favelas* and it would be just another day.

> *My samba says*
> *And I believe*
> *No one can be happy*
> *Without pain...*

THE FRUSTRATED COLOSSUS

CHAPTER 7

Rio's only rival in any contest for the title 'Most Stylish City in South America' would be Buenos Aires. But our karate-black-belted surfer camera assistant was less than overwhelmed by his welcome in the Argentine capital. Travel in the southern cone of South America had been easier than we had been used to in the north and it was some time since we had had need of Marc's services as a human car-jack, but in Buenos Aires it was not long before he was challenged to a trial of strength. It happened like this. Marc was walking along the pavement of Esmeralda Street when a bus squeezed past from behind him, overhanging the pavement. The side of the bus caught Marc by the shoulder, rubbed and bumped and spun him, and left him in its wake, still standing but panting. And boiling with indignation! After all, Marc had been walking properly on the pavement, the bus had had no right... and Marc was off after that bus. The streets of BA are laid out as a grid; lots of cross roads to slow the bus. Marc sprinted after it, along Esmeralda, across Tucuman, across Viamonte, across Avenida Paraguay, until at Cordoba he caught up, miming to the driver through the window what had happened. But the driver turned up his nose and pulled away. The dark Australian on the pavement was of no importance, it seemed, beneath contempt. Marc walked on: Can't win 'em all.

Further along Esmeralda he saw a chance of consolation — a pretty girl, a *Porteña* as natives of Buenos Aires are called. Marc asked for direction, and the pretty *Porteña* took the bait and walked on with him. Now, deep in conversation, Marc overtook the bus without realising it, where it was held up at the crossing of Esmeralda and Alvear. And then — half a block along Santa Fe — the juggernaut struck again: Whack! Marc's head jerked as the aggressor's side mirror smacked him from behind. The driver had skilfully aimed his bus to infuriate but not to wound.

Muttering to his new friend that he'd be back, Marc was off down Santa Fe after his assailant. A favourite word of his was 'powering' and powering he was. Surfer's lungs rushed oxygen to racing legs as Marc sprinted after that bus. By the time it was approaching Suipacha, Marc was alongside: karate-hardened hands chopped at the side panels as he advanced along the enemy towards the front and He Who Must Die — the driver. By the time Marc had drummed his way to the front of the bus, the driver knew his hour had come. No more games of hit-and-run on the streets of Buenos Aires, no more leering down at his victims; he was destined now for Chacaritas, BA's vast city-of-the-dead cemetery. And, misfortune upon catastrophe, there was a bus stop ahead, with a queue waiting to delay him and deliver him up to the terrible apocalypse of a young man pounding on his now frail-seeming cab. Like a captain going down with his ship, the driver put duty before his own life and stopped by the bus queue.

In a moment he must open the hydraulic doors and Marc would be on him. The driver's hand was on the lever... But then, like a captain reaching for his lifebelt at the last moment, the driver hesitated. Outside, would-be passengers looked up at him from behind the terrible hands of Marc, now threatening to tear the doors open; inside, would-be pedestrians stood waiting to get off. The driver sweated. He grabbed that lifebelt — self-preservation triumphed over duty. Without ever opening the door he let in the clutch and roared away, sweating with relief as the thumps of Marc's pounding hands receded along the side of the escaping bus. And Marc? Then and there he made up his mind about Argentina: 'Argentina Sux!'

As the frustrated bus queue watched an even more frustrated Marc, they might have sympathised. The Argentinians are a people well experienced in frustration. They have had years of watching their country fail to fulfil its apparent potential, years of watching wealth turn into poverty, years of watching Argentina become, like Marc at that moment, a frustrated colossus.

Their capital, Buenos Aires, was everything you might expect of the capital of a country which by 1945 had been one of the ten richest in the world. Tree-lined avenues, Belle Epoque buildings, stately parks. You could think you were in Europe, and that was really what they wanted you to think. Buenos Aires seemed a city of French architecture, full of Italians who spoke Spanish and thought they were English. Once, when someone had commented on the poor state of the nation's economy, an Argentinian was said to have replied 'Yes, but we're not as badly off as the **rest** of Europe'.

(Page 140) Branding on the Argentine Pampas.

Confused about its identity, Argentina was nevertheless still the best educated, most urbanised nation in South America. 'God is everywhere' they said, 'But He rules from Buenos Aires'. But if he did, he'd been doing a poor job. A nation that had once seemed destined for greatness had fallen on hard times. There had been military dictatorships, an atrocious near-civil war in which the young had seemed to go mad and had been obliterated, a humiliating defeat in a war over some offshore islands, and now, though democratic government had returned, the economy was in a shambles. Inflation had been as high as six hundred per cent; there were more zeros on the banknotes than the eye could count.

What had gone wrong? Why had the Argentinians turned a prosperous past into a confused present? Was there some flaw in the people? The philosopher Ortega y Gasset had once written of Argentina: 'The horizon is forever making gestures of abundance. Scarcely anyone is where he is but in advance of himself. And from **there** he governs his life **here,** his real present life. Everyone lives as though his dreams of the future were already reality'.

That overconfidence was reflected in something which other South Americans said about the Argentinians, whom they generally disliked as arrogant and overbearing: 'What's the quickest way to make a fortune?' they sneered. 'Easy. Just buy an Argentinian for what he's worth, then sell him for what he **thinks** he's worth.'

But, if Argentinians were blinded to reality by pride, their president certainly wasn't. We went to the Pink House for an audience with President Alfonsin and found him relaxed, humorous, and realistic. His Spanish was spiced with *Lunfado* — the Italian-Spanish dialect of his capital. I put it to him that Argentina was not at all the stable and prosperous place it had once seemed destined to be. 'Ah!' he joked. 'So you've noticed'. There was no 'side' to this Argentinian, and he made no bones about the mess his country was in, with its giant debts, its seething unrest, and its frustrated ambitions.

Asking other eminent Argentinians what had gone wrong proved to be a hazardous pastime, not because they were hostile to such questions — they weren't at all — but because people were so hospitable. 'I wonder if you could spare me some time to discuss...' you would request on the phone. 'Ah yes, of course', they would answer. 'Come and have lunch'.

'Lunch' seemed to be the first thing an Argentinian said after 'Hello'. To research in Buenos Aires was to become fat. But you did get answers. And you found that people certainly were exasperated and frustrated by the failure of their nation. 'What's wrong is that we're immigrants' suggested a lady at a luncheon for twenty or so guests in an elegant private house. 'All that people want to do here is to make enough money for a house and a car. No real ambition. Mind you', she went on, spooning Italian food from English silver, 'I work hard on our farm up in the north. Have to — the economy's so crazy: Do you know that not long ago a pair of shoes was worth more than two cows?'

'Too many military governments' explained another guest. 'Awful people! I wouldn't want to see anyone in our family joining the military!'

(Left) BA — Europe in South America.

(Above and below) The streets of Buenos Aires.

(above) President Alfonsin trying to heal a nation's wounds.

(left) Carlos Gardel and admirer. Fifty years in the grave but they say he sings better every day.

'These officers spent so much on themselves when they were in power' complained another as the butler served great dishes of the beef without which no Argentinian feels he's eaten at all 'Look at the fine houses those jumped-up soldiers took over as army clubs'.

Over coffee, still pressing my enquiries as to what it was in the Argentinians which had derailed their country, I got from my hostess a reply which was perhaps not so evasive as it at first seemed. 'Young man', she told me, taking my arm and leading me briskly towards the music room, 'You'll never understand Argentina until you learn to dance the tango!' A grand piano filled the room with passionate music, and she propelled me into the national dance. I began to learn about the tango and perhaps about the Argentinians too. Theirs was a dance utterly different from all others in South America — a dance which did seem to have grown out of that same over-bearing pretentiousness which had annoyed the philosopher Ortega y Gasset and had provoked the people who joked about trading in overproud Argentinians. I enjoyed my stumbling attempt at the tango, I enjoyed still more watching it executed by Argentinians. But what did the dance say of the Argentinians, with its haughty thrusts of the chin and its contemptuous strutting? What it spoke of seemed to be arrogance and self-absorption. Self-absorption was the essence of the tango. Above all, the dancers had to keep their expressions aloof and fixed; there must be no meeting of each other's eyes, no sign of affection. And the tango was important to Argentinians: in the recent election campaign it had been stressed that Alfonsin was a good *tangista* — and therefore a true son of the nation. And when one great tango star had died they'd given him almost a state funeral; Carlos Gardel was his name and he was still idolised now fifty years later. The tango truly was a dance which seemed to emphasise the very qualities which detractors of Argentina identified as its besetting weakness. The trouble with the Argentinians, they said, was that they were too arrogant and cocksure ever to face their problems realistically, and too self-centred ever to unite and tackle them.

Disunity, many people had told us, was one of the causes of the nation's failure. And certainly there was potential for disunity amongst the Argentinians: they were a nation of quite recent immigrants with widely differing roots. Originally there had been Indians and then Spanish *conquistadores*. But much later had come Italians, British, Negroes, Jugoslavs, Germans and more Spanish. From this mix the Indians and the blacks had been eliminated: the blacks had been used as cannon-fodder in so many local wars that, by the end of the nineteenth century, they were fading away. And the Indians had been wiped out in the same century by a comprehensive campaign of genocide. But, if the removal of those two most visibly separate races from the population had been expected to help it unite, no such thing had happened. Argentina had remained a nation of different peoples. Such a rich mix could have its advantages, of course. But in the Argentinians, given their inclination towards self-centredness, it had tended to produce not one united nation but an assortment of different people who just happened to occupy the same country.

(Above and opposite)
Porteños — the citizens
of BA.

Pursuing the theme of disunity as one of the causes of Argentina's frustration, we went to look at two of its self-contained peoples. First, the British. The British community in Argentina is the largest outside the Commonwealth. The British had contributed much to the shaping of the nation. They had brought to the country its banks, its railways, its gas and electricity, its meat-packing, its first steamship, its first sheep-dip, its first wire fence. But we had brought our snobbery too and the apparatus of our divisive class system. The Jockey Club, with its marble halls and air of crushing exclusivity, seemed still to belong in nineteenth century Pall Mall rather than in Buenos Aires. Its aloofness had been clearly recognised by the working-class hordes of Peronists who had rushed to burn down the club's original quarters as soon as they had their first taste of power. The Hurlingham Club, too, set amidst beautiful polo fields, was another formidably British institution, with mock-tudorish club rooms where *The Field* and *Horse and Hound* still waited in their leather binders. The Hurlingham had had to relax its Britishness a little and, as one member put it, 'These days we even have Spanish-speaking members'. But institutions like the Jockey Club and the Hurlingham are not the kind which you would set up if you wanted to foster a united spirit among Argentinians. Such clubs are created for the opposite purpose — to maintain the separateness of one group. They recall the days, only a generation ago, when some British Argentinians considered it beneath them to speak Spanish or to have it taught to their children. And so does a school we visited — St George's College. True, they do speak Spanish there, and out on the cricket pitches beyond the chapel the talk is of *Boleando* and *batteando*, and *fieldeando;* and true this archetypal English public school in a suburb of Buenos Aires now opens its doors a little wider to admit — besides a scion of the Hapsburgs — the son of the cocaine king of Bolivia; but St George's is a bastion of an English way of doing things, not of any Argentine way. One disenchanted old-boy said that the school was divisive not only vertically (in dividing a British-orientated group from the rest of Argentinians), but also horizontally in that it encouraged in its pupils an elitist notion that they had been born to be at the top of Argentine society, and were not required to develop either the leadership or the sense of responsibility to the lower levels of that society which might help to unite it.

Leaving behind the pillars of the Argentine British, we went down the social ladder and, seemingly, across national frontiers to see another of the peoples who make up the un-united nation — the Italians. In the la Boca quarter of Buenos Aires, around the old docks the cafes dreamed of Italy: the 'Torna a Sorrento'; the 'Bella Napoli'; 'Genaro's'. By the harbour a violinist played tangoes interspersed with the melodies of Italy. We walked with an old man, Don Vicente, who showed us the quay where in 1923 he'd got off the ship from Italy. He had arrived hoping to find work so that his wife and daughter could follow him from Italy to his new country. Like many of the Italians who had come to Argentina he was from the harsh south, from Calabria. Great waves of Italians had begun coming over in the 1870s and they had continued to come. Later, when Argentina had begun to industrialise, the Italians together with the

(Right) Italian immigrants poured in through the docks at La Boca.

unemployed from Northern Spain had presented the country with a ready-made working class. But a foreign working class. By the time Don Vicente had arrived half the population of Buenos Aires was from abroad; a third of all Argentinians were people who had been born elsewhere. Had Don Vicente and his fellow immigrants really become Argentinians? Had their sons and daughters? With the old man we went to a procession of the Society of the Virgin of Grace. The language used everywhere was not the national tongue — Spanish — but Lunfado, the Italo-Spanish dialect which spiced the conversation of President Alfonsin. The flavour of the procession was Italian — when they had carried their virgin around the district and back into the church they would dance tarantellas in the street. Their names were all Italian. Here, even second and third generation Argentinians had names like Luciano and Massiano. Walking beside a Massiano in the procession I asked him, 'How long have you been in this country?' 'I was born here' he shouted above the wail of the band. 'And are you an Argentinian?' 'No', he shouted, without hesitation, 'No, I am Italian!'

Argentina seemed to be a nation in need of cement. Full of peoples who were clinging to their widely different roots and who were blinded by self-absorption to the possibility of uniting, it was no wonder the country was failing. What could hold it all together? What ever had? In South America the most common cement for divided nations had been dictatorship. And Argentina had had its share of those *caudillos*, those

(Above) The Hurlingham Club (Buenos Aires) — 'frightfully British'.

(Left) Polo at the Hurlingham.

(Right) Sports day at St George's College, BA.

strong men. From 1835 till 1852 one of them — Juan Manuel Rosas — had ruled the volatile nation from Buenos Aires. The cement he'd used had been the vision of a unified people, applied with the typical ruthlessness of a dictator. Lesser leaders who had tried to go their own way had their heads severed and raised on poles. Everyone in the capital had to wear red to show support for Rosas. His portrait was everywhere, even on church altars. But, classically, the type of men who become dictators do not encourage younger men around them to develop in stature to the point where they might succeed the dictator and advance his cause. So when Rosas' brutal enforcement of unity ended, there was no one to take over his cause of cementing Argentina into a united nation.

Later there had developed a certain myth which had provided at least a smear of cement for the Argentinians. It was a national symbol which everyone had been prepared to agree stood for being Argentinian — the great Argentine *gaucho*.

Out on the endless pampas, where the wealth of Argentina was, and where many believed that the nation's soul resided, we went to watch *gauchos* at work. Already we had seen something of the uniting power of the *gaucho* ideal at a rally in the city of Lujan. Thousands of Argentinians with horses had travelled there from the length of the country to parade dressed as *gauchos*. It was an event marked by prayers and appeals for a uniting of the nation which was to be brought about by a renaissance of the *gaucho* spirit. It was a formidable display. The National Federation of the Gaucho took over the city to honour the concept of the *gaucho*.

(Below) Would-be gauchos at Lujan.

154

Mounted on a fine horse and dressed in the high boots, baggy *bombacha* pants, black hat and jacket, and silver belt and spurs of the Federation, its chairman — a former General of the Air Force and president of the national airline — expounded to me the *gaucho* ideal as the cement which Argentina needed: self-reliance, ruggedness, dash, independence! All Argentinians must unite, he told me, and because that was so important the Federation was even allowing Italians to join. He didn't much like the 'spaghettis' — Argentina had too many of them. But unity was more important than anything else now.

A few days later, more than a thousand kilometres away, we arrived at the home of the men on whom the *gaucho* myth was based. The ones we had come to see worked on an impeccably English cattle farm, Ita Caabo. This *estancia* was so English it had once been visited by the last Prince of Wales and still had the English bed and chairs imported for the royal comfort. The *estancia* manager, John Adams, proudly introduced us to his thirty stockmen. They were the present day inheritors of the *gaucho* tradition, and they certainly were impressive. They were men made of leather, magnificent horsemen, impressive products of a tradition of toughness in which dignity was earned by hard work and competence. To watch these descendants of the *gauchos* whispering orders to a paddockful of horses (each man used four horses) which lined themselves up like guardsmen, was to understand why the *gaucho* was so cherished by the Argentinians as a national symbol. He cuts a romantic figure. A nation of men as tough and as disciplined as the *gaucho* might well become a nation of proud achievers. But watching these men riding off into the sunset, we remembered that they themselves were a dying breed: 'Among the last you'll see', said the manager. And anyway, from the point of view of unifying a nation the *gauchos* were no more than a symbol, and symbols could do very little. A pleasure though it was to see these legendary men, our search for the causes of Argentina's frustration was advanced not by them but by one remark from the *estancia's* manager. Argentine agriculture was not in a good state, he told us, and the reason he gave was one which fitted in with the idea put forward by the philosopher and echoed in the joke about overproud Argentinians. The Argentinians had been too complacent, he said, they'd failed to realise that they weren't still living in the easy days when all it took to make a fortune was a spread of pampas and some cattle. They'd sat back full of deluded confidence while the land had wasted around them. Now Argentina, with some of the richest land in the world, supported fewer cattle per hectare than did Denmark with some of the poorest. What Argentinians needed now was not symbols but a dose of realism. 'And discipline as well,' added his colleague watching the quiet efficiency of the *gauchos* rounding up stock. 'I'm a third generation Argentinian, but I have to say that as a nation we've no discipline: We just do whatever we want; if a traffic light's not green we all assume it's broken.'

He seemed to be appealing for a strong leader — another Rosas. Was dictatorship the only cement for Argentina? They had had a famous dictator through the 'forties and 'fifties, of course, a man who had become the most world-famous leader in the history of South America:

(Above, right, below and facing page) A powerful myth — thousands travel to Lujan for the annual rally of the National Federation of the Gaucho.

Juan Peron had come to power as one of a group of officers which ousted a failing elected government in order that Argentina should fulfill its destiny. 'Argentina should become', said Peron and his colleagues, 'the Colossus of the South'. He was quick to see a power base. The working masses had no party to represent them, and as a military attache in Mussolini's Italy, Peron had seen what could be done with a crowd. The masses of Argentina were looking for a new style of *caudillo*, of strongman, and Peron made himself their idol. He had the qualities of a *caudillo* — masculine charm, dash, eloquence, the common touch. And Argentina swiftly fell under the spell of this slick and glossy man. Friend of successful racing drivers, footballers, boxers, husband of a glamorous actress, Eva, he was in effect the ultimate tango dancer. Peron took Argentina as his partner and seduced her. He would be sweeping, he would be masterful, he would do with her whatever he wanted and Argentina would surrender to him. She would tolerate his lies, his cheating, his corruption, and even though she would eventually send him away into exile, she would find it impossible to live without him and she would bring him back. And even after he died she would go on loving Peron and voting for whoever she thought had inherited his mantle.

This is not to say that Peron achieved nothing solid. In his early years in politics he did in effect enfranchise the workers and make a blue collar something to be proud of, and he did succeed in winning the presidency in an open and fair election. He created jobs for the middle class by inflating the bureaucracy, he opened up the universities to them, industrialized the nation, and won a loyalty from a wide cross-section of Argentinians which has lasted right up to the present day. But Argentina's besotted failure to reject him when he became corrupt and manifestly hollow, and her infatuation with him for at least a decade after his death tended to confirm our growing diagnosis — that Argentinians had been afflicted with a severe case of unrealism. It showed in the worship of Peron, in the vanity which prompted the joke about overvalued Argentinians, in the reliance on a symbol — the *gaucho,* in the complacency about the declining cattle industry.

In the years since Peron Argentinians have been on a roller coaster of elected governments and military coups, and they have been through a ghastly near-civil war. And that catastrophe has raised new divisions which seem unlikely to be bridged for many years to come. In the famous Plaza de Mayo in front of the Pink House, mothers of some of the ten thousand young people who disappeared in the Dirty War were still holding their weekly protests. It was hard to imagine how they could ever be reconciled with the military. After what had happened to their children, these mothers and the families they represented were inevitably inconsolable. It made little difference to them that the military governments which had been responsible for the wholesale torture and murder of their sons and daughters had gone, finally discredited in that deluded war over a handful of islands when the generals showed that not only could they not make the economy work, but neither could they succeed at the job they existed for — war. It made little difference to the bereaved mothers that a new president had been democratically elected. It made

(Above, left and facing page) Gauchos and their horses still work Ita Caabo. They are 'among the last you'll see'.

(Left) Peronist rally
— blind faith and loaded
coshes.

little difference that his commissioners were seeking vigorously to confirm the deaths of the disappeared and to find the guilty. The Mothers of the Plaza de Mayo would never be reconciled to the slaughter of their children — and would never tolerate the many Argentinians who argued that the deaths had been necessary to the survival of the nation itself.

The prospects for Argentina, with such a history of division and of delusion, did not seem good. President Alfonsin spoke purposefully of uniting the nation to clean up the mess, of confronting Argentina's huge debts, and of moving ahead at last. You felt the Argentinians were fortunate to have a decent man in power at last. But few people outside the President's own circle gave him much hope of survival. They pointed out that to complete his term of office he would have to become the first elected president for sixty years not to be ousted by the army. The military, they said, were already massing in the wings.

Our last evening in Buenos Aires was spent at a rally of the Peronist Party. It gave no cause for optimism. If the Peronists ever had a political philosophy — a policy — they no longer did: they were no longer a political party but a blind faith. But they were many: half the seats in the country were still Peronist. And, to judge from this rally, they had little to offer Argentina in the way of realism. The rally took place in a football stadium and was a gathering of thugs. Everywhere drums were dully, brutishly thudded, not with drumsticks but with lengths of loaded hosepipe. And as the drums were coshed into sullen thunder, young Peronists in black leather created a vision of chaos. They started fires in the packed stands, they hurled tear gas grenades which panicked the crowd into dangerous stampedes, they urged you to jump up and down for Peronism or be beaten up, they howled with approval or derision — it was impossible to tell which — and drowned the manic exhortations of leaders who could be glimpsed but not heard giving messianic speeches from a platform behind the clouds of gas.

Realism was nowhere to be seen. Aggression and frustration were everywhere. It seemed an all too appropriate note on which to leave the Frustrated Colossus.

A BETTER MAÑANA

CHAPTER 8

Travel the world and you probably won't find a country more beautiful and varied than Colombia. Travel South America and you probably won't find a people more vital than the Colombians. It is said that Colombia is South America writ large — a caricature of the continent. And so it is. But not only in beauty and vitality: Colombia has a history of violence unequalled anywhere else in South America, with four guerilla armies, murder squads, mafia killings and street robbers who will kill you for your wallet. Colombia has profound inequality, with much of its beautiful territory in the hands of a fortunate few while the many have little. And Colombia has foreign exploitation, with too much dependence on too few products whose prices are controlled elsewhere. ¶But if Colombia has both the curses and the blessings of South America — both the beauty and vivacity as well as the crime, corruption, exploitation, illiteracy, inequality, violence, poverty and hunger — Colombia also has something else as well, a president who is trying to tackle those evils. He is an honest and vigorous man who, in his turbulent caricature of a country, is trying to confront all the enduring problems of South America. ¶The name of this man who is attempting miracles is Belisario Betancur. When we met him he had been President of Colombia for two years with two more to go.

In Colombia no President may serve two consecutive terms, so 'BB' as he was known had just four years in which to try and do something about problems which had tormented most of South America for centuries. We decided that if we followed him in some of his efforts, the result for us might be a fitting conclusion to our researches and to our travels.

Belisario Betancur was a peasant President. He had grown up as one of a large family in a rough cottage in a region known for its coal and coffee. As a boy he had picked coffee before doing his homework and later when he won a place at the university, away in the city, he sometimes slept in the park to make his funds stretch. His education took him eventually to the London School of Economics. Paradoxically from that renowned bastion of left-of-centre ideas, he went home to Colombia and joined the Conservatives. By the time he won the Colombian Presidency in 1982, he had built up wide support, and he was voted into office with a record poll. He was still a Conservative but, paradoxically again, his platform was reform. By 1983, opinion polls were showing that ninety-two per cent of Colombians supported his policies, though it has to be said that his support always fluctuated drastically with the economy. By the end of his first two years in office, he had been awarded a peace prize in Spain, he had appealed to both super powers to stop meddling in South America and, with a speech which reduced the United Nations to tears, he had begun to become something which Latin America has seldom if ever had — a spokesman for all its peoples.

We visited the birthplace of this unusual man. On a green hillside the Colombian flag, red, yellow and blue, hung beside the small peasant cottage. On the wall was a stone plaque. It described Belisario Betancur as 'the light and hope of the nation'. The President himself was against plaques. He had asked people not to hang them up when he visited, but that hadn't stopped people here expressing the feelings they had for the man. And Colombians can be poetic even about politics. Beside the plaque were scrawled some lines of graffiti: someone had written, 'In this humble place was born the intelligence and the heart that made the leap from here to the Nariño Palace'.

Named for an early statesman, the Nariño Palace is the residence of Colombia's presidents in the capital, Bogota. Inside, in a hall behind the palace's rather pretty Georgian pillars and porticoes, we looked at a collection of paintings. Every one was Colombian and that, we learned, was a matter of policy. The President invited Colombia's leading artists and sculptors to lend their work to the palace which he then opened to the public. This was a small part of his campaign to build pride in his people. Betancur wanted to end their tendency to bow before everything which came from the great exporter of Coca-Cola culture across the Caribbean.

Touring the current art collection with us, the President paused in front of a vast painting of Simon Bolivar. The 'Liberator' was addressing the nineteenth century senate of a Colombia newly freed from the domination of a super power at that time — Spain. Bolivar had tried to bring about what he called 'the revolution for which the people are waiting', but Bolivar had discovered how hard it was to change South

(Page 164) Angel — Colombian coffee worker with the traditional carrie bag of his region.

America. Gloomily the Liberator had concluded, 'He who serves the revolution here is ploughing the sea. South America is ungovernable'. I put it to President Betancur that if a man as great as Bolivar had felt so crushed by the problems of South America, wasn't BB discouraged? With a good humour which proved to be typical of him, the President put that in proportion: 'Even Bolivar had his off days!' he laughed. 'I've no doubt that when the Liberator said that, he'd been going through a difficult time. We all have those you know, but we have to do our best. But of course', he admitted, turning serious, 'it isn't easy to change things. Our problems are rooted very deep'.

The problems of South America. We began to travel through Belisario's land, from problem to problem rather as a tourist would go from beauty spot to beauty spot. From Bogota we crossed one of the *cordillera* — one of the three northern arms of the Andes — to the lush green hills where they grow what any Colombian will tell you is the finest coffee this side of paradise. Our home for a week was 'La Loma', a fine old house of deep verandahs and shaded gardens, commanding a great *hacienda* — an estate given over to coffee. At La Loma, as we rode through a green land of hills luxuriant with coffee bushes, we were in the presence of one of the great problems which any man who would reform South America must face. All the land we were crossing belonged to one family. Most of the good land in Colombia belonged to a handful of people. Back in the 'sixties there had been an attempt to change that with a bill called 'The Colombian Agrarian Social Reform Act'. Fine words for a feeble law. It affected only one quarter of one per cent of the cultivable land. Often,

*(Above and below left)
On the slopes of the
Colombian Andes.*

*(Right) Guard at the
President's Nariño
Palace.*

*(Below) For the Colombian
sun.*

*(Above) The home of
Angel the coffee worker.*

when land reform has been tried in South America it has been done
ineffectually. It has been introduced, usually only in response to pressure, by an unwilling oligarchy. And since it was their own land they were
losing, the members of such power groups were naturally more concerned to sabotage land reform than to make it work. It is an abiding fact
of South American life that attempts at land reform nearly always end up
with real control remaining in the hands of the landed few. And in most
of the continent it hasn't even been tried: land reform is for *mañana.*

What that means was all around us at La Loma. There were nearly
three hundred peope living on the estate, the coffee workers and their
families, and almost everything they had — their jobs, their homes, even
their school — was on land which belonged to one person. On him they
were dependent. They were part of that pattern which makes South
America a rich land full of poor people, and in their case the imbalance
was accentuated because the owner of La Loma happened to be a child
— a boy of no more than ten years old. The child did not actually run the
estate — that was done by trustees. But that anyone should receive such
wealth and (when he reached twenty-one) such power over the lives of
others, without having to do a hand's turn to earn them seemed a fine
symbol of the inequity of South America. While millions might go
hungry, a boy could inherit the earth. And yet, as I rode up to the estate

school and listened to the children of the coffee workers singing, I had to acknowledge a paradox: however low their station in the national hierarchy, these children of peasants knew that there was in Colombia one man who had started out like them, and in even less egalitarian times than theirs, yet who had been able to become President. But then I reflected that BB's leap from cottage to palace was really just the exception which proved the rule — that the gulf between rich and poor was so wide as to be almost uncrossable. And no reformer could try to break the rich's hold on the land without arousing the opposition of the powerful. It was a key to reform, and it was something which BB would have to do if he was really to bring about a more equitable society.

Another key to reform was there to be seen at La Loma in that school. In the President's view there could never be a truly participatory democracy until everyone was well enough educated to be able to understand the issues of the day. He had launched a literacy programme called Project Bolivar. The idea was that all over Colombia every high school student should teach someone to read. And here in the country school, the aim was to narrow the gap in literacy between country and town. No more than seventy per cent of Colombians could read and write, and the proportion was higher in the cities than in the country. Schools were rarer in the countryside, and they faced special difficulties. Typically, education for the children at La Loma tended to be interrupted by parents who wanted them to help on the coffee slopes: the more coffee you picked, the higher your pay, so every hand counted. But school was compulsory in theory and, under Betancur, it was becoming more so in practice. I remembered meeting a priest who had observed that some Latin American governments seemed content to ignore education, believing perhaps that an illiterate people would be more easily led and exploited. 'Talk about literacy programmes,' the priest had said disgustedly, 'Some of those governments have **ill**iteracy programmes!'

'A, B, C' sang the children at La Loma. It made you wonder who would one day pick the coffee if all these children grew up literate and able to seek more elevated work. But you couldn't doubt that education was a stepping stone towards a more equitable society.

The children's fathers, outside working on the coffee slopes, were unwittingly embroiled in another of South America's great problems — the one-product economy. We watched one of the coffee-pickers working with implacable patience and leathery endurance. Angel was his name, and the coffee beans in his calloused hands were the symbol of a bad bargain. The history of coffee is the history of South Americans losing out in world markets. By the time those coffee beans in Angel's hand reached a supermarket shelf in the developed world, virtually everyone concerned in the trade would probably have made more money from it than the Colombians. In the 1960s more money was made by foreign governments **taxing** Colombian coffee than Colombia itself made from **growing** it. And fluctuations in price, determined by cartels abroad, often sent shock waves through the economy. One year Colombians would find they could buy an imported tractor with ten sacks of their coffee, but in the next year it would need fifty sacks.

(Above) Angel the coffee
worker.

(Left) Coffee slopes at
La Loma.

(Above right) Mountain
woman.

(Right) The Foreman.

And to workers, like Angel, it had meant that whether or not they could afford to ask some *campesina* 'Will you marry me?' could depend on decisions made by foreign cartels. The Colombians might grow the best coffee crop in history but have very little to show for it if the brokers overseas said so. It was the same story of too much dependence and too little control which we had seen with Bolivia's tin and Chile's nitrates and copper. How to change it? Belisario Betancur was encouraging the coffee growers to seek wider markets and generate more competition. But more important was diversification. If South America could produce a greater variety of exports, countries would not find their economic systems so vulnerable to plunging world prices. Colombia was developing its exports of cotton, oil, meat and tobacco. And now, more importantly, a giant coal project was under way which was calculated to overtake coffee's export earnings by the year 1990.

On the day we left La Loma a party was held in the old coffee sorting factory. A pig was killed and, as if drawn by its dying squeals, the coffee workers appeared from their cottages. They wore their best machetes, and those who could afford them wore *carriels* — the elaborate shoulder bags in which the men of that region carry the necessities of survival. One of the best dressed was Angel, the man we had watched at work. With a bottle in one hand and his wife in the other, Angel danced a fine *cumbia.* A trio of coffee workers sang tenderly as the setting sun turned the hills a delicate red. Listening to the words of their song I was struck, not for the first time in South America, by the easy acceptance of violence. In their daily dealings with each other the South Americans often display a warmth which makes us Anglo-Saxons seem frozen by comparison. Smile for smile they show more warmth to each other in a day than many of us do in a year. But their spontaneity also allows them to explode into violence more freely than we do. They can swing from embraces to knives with startling ease. In the song they were singing now, both moods were present. The singer, his face suffused with tenderness, was addressing some woman who had left him; his heart was breaking, he sobbed, he couldn't bear to lose her, he begged her to return, please please, otherwise — oh dear — he would slice her face with a razor, gouge out her eyes and her navel, and murder her mother!

That volatile viciousness, apparently unrestrained by the tenderness which South Americans so often show, seemed a significant part of life throughout the continent. And in Colombia — caricature of South America — past violence had played a terrible part in shaping the present. In 1948 there had begun in Colombia what became known as *La Violenca* — The Violence. It began with a riot in the capital and grew into a national blood bath which lasted for more than nine years. It began with politics — Conservatives against Liberals. One man — the leader of the Liberals — was assassinated, and a tide of violence swept the capital. In the first two days five or six thousand bodies were heaped against the cemetery walls. *La Violencia* spread from Bogota to the countryside and there it took root. *La Violencia* became an undeclared civil war which lasted more than a decade. By the time it ended, the dead numbered about one hundred and eighty thousand.

(Left) 'I'll slice your face
and gouge out your
navel...'

(Overleaf) School bus —
Antioquia, Colombia.

One story gives a sense of the awfulness of Colombia's *Violencia:* a bus filled with children from a music academy — the conservatorium — was on its way through the mountains when it was stopped on the road by an armed group of Liberal supporters. 'Who are you all? Where are you from?'

'We're from the conservatorium', explained the children's teacher. And that was it. The word 'conservatorium' sounded altogether too Conservative to the Liberals. They machine-gunned every child on the bus.

Though the rivals in *La Violencia* called themselves Liberals and Conservatives, it was not really a war between political parties. In the 1890s a President had said 'Colombia has no parties; only hereditary hatreds'. And so it was. In 1948 when *La Violencia* erupted, every little town had its local *caudillo,* and its bitter memories from the previous century which had seen a civil war in every decade. *La Violencia* was private violence and village vendetta legitimised by political labels. For more than nine years, family fought family, village fought village, and Colombia was turned into a graveyard. A bishop known as 'The Hammer of the Heretics' urged his flock to go out and kill Protestants; killers cut the throats of their victims then pulled their tongues out through the wound to make what was known as *la corbata* (the necktie); fields and crops were left deserted as whole villages fled to the cities for safety.

La Violencia was an explosion of that violence which never seems far below the surface of South America, and it was an explosion whose fallout is still troubling Colombia, and setting problems for any reforming President. Now, twenty-five years after *La Violencia,* the cities are still swollen by the hundreds of thousands who had fled the violent countryside. Their numbers made Colombia's cities even more unmanageable than others in South America. Rio, Lima, Buenos Aires, Sao Paulo, La Paz, Santiago were overcrowded, but they had been packed by nothing worse than the general urban drift of the previous twenty years. But the cities of Colombia had taken an extra burden of millions of refugees from terror. And many of them had been twisted by the experiences. Human life had come to be seen as cheap, and the children of *La Violencia* — children who perhaps had seen their parents mutilated — now became willing recruits to the Mafia and to bands of guerillas who grew to become a power in the land with their armed campaigns for reform.

By the time Belisario Betancur took office there were no fewer than four guerilla armies operating out of Colombia's vast jungles. One of the best known — M19 — was said to be armed by Ghadaffi's Libya. Three Libyan freight planes, loaded with crates of guns marked 'Famine Relief' and bound for Betancur's land, had been discovered when they'd stopped to refuel in Brazil. Another guerilla army was insisting that it would not lay down its weapons until there was land reform. There seemed to be no answer to Colombia's guerillas. Once, in the 'sixties, the army had got on top of them for a time, helped by American 'military advisers' who had been despatched to Colombia in the fear that it might become another Cuba. But by the time Belisario Betancur took office, the guerillas seemed unstoppable. He had tried an unusual and controversial approach — an amnesty — and was having some success. But

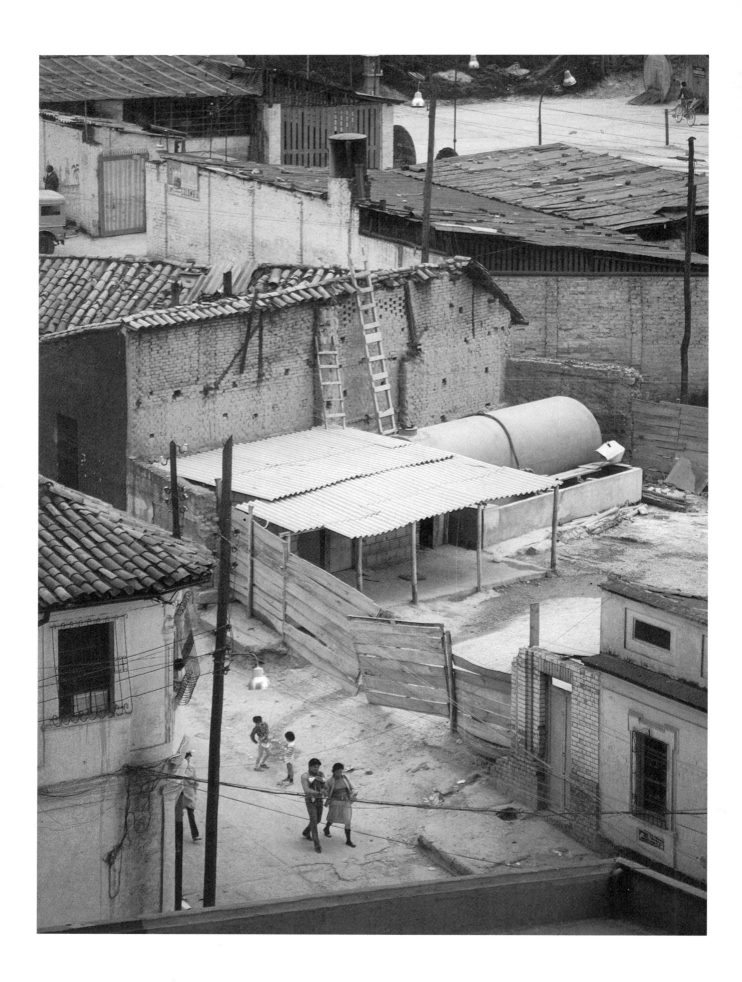

there were problems. Some guerillas freed from prison in the amnesty simply went back to the jungle, and that infuriated the military which had sweated to capture them; other guerillas did give up their political cause, but finding there was little work for unemployed guerillas they turned to crime. They had used kidnapping as a way of fund-raising for their undercover armies, now they used it for themselves. At one school for the children of the rich, a whole class was kidnapped.

The President was keeping his amnesty open but was preparing the army for more action if necessary. We watched a regiment of commandos training in the jungle. 'I am a *Lancero*' shouted a young soldier going through his final test: we held our breath because he was clambering perilously along narrow girders, high above a bridge. Now as he hopped from rivet to rivet he was chanting the regimental code.

'Loyalty, valour and sacrifice' the young soldier shouted, swaying precariously on the topmost beams.

> *Loyalty, valour and sacrifice —*
> *Three words that I shall keep.*
> *I am a Lancero and the service calls.*
> *I am willing to die for my country!*

Next he was hanging by his hands from a beam stuck out above the coffee-coloured river some thirteen metres below waiting for the command to jump — 'Yes, my Colonel', he shouted when it came, and let go to plummet to the water far below. Further up the river more advanced *Lanceros* were making running jumps from a thirty-three metre cliff.

The army was well trained to confront Colombia's guerillas, and it was not pleased with Betancur's amnesty. Any army becomes alarmed when leniency is shown to its enemies, and the frustration of the Colombian army had already found a vicious outlet long before Belisario had come to power. Soldiers disguised in plain clothes had taken the law into their own hands and were operating as death squads, murdering whomever they judged to be their enemies. A lawyer who had defended guerilla suspects was one of their victims. Betancur had taken the risky step of confronting the army and ordering the prosecution of the generals behind the murder squads. But he had been frustrated by a Supreme Court decision to hand the accused over to be tried by their fellow officers. And now he was risking a worse confrontation with his army by offering amnesty to their enemies. It was many years since there had been a military coup in Colombia, but the risk was always there. A quotation which I came across summed it up. It was from George Pendle's *A History of Latin America* and it said: 'Betancourt — always a social reformer at heart — was faced with the problem that has baffled many democratic Latin American leaders: how can social reforms be effected by parliamentary methods when the armed forces disapprove?' It applied exactly to Belisario Betancur in 1984. But ironically it had been written about a different Betancourt — Romulo, President of Venezuela — a quarter of a century before. BB was indeed facing one of the enduring problems of South America.

Another of Colombia's problems which had been made worse by *La Violencia* was crime. The migration away from the country violence into the already overcrowded cities had led to years of hardship, and the resulting acute poverty and family break-ups had thrown thousands of young people onto the streets. They had become the *gamines* — the famous street robbers of Colombia. 'Don't wear watches or jewellery, take your glasses off if you can see without them, and NEVER walk in a crowd' warned *The South American Handbook*.

In downtown Bogota in an open-sided cafe where the bar stools were chained to the floor we met some of those young criminals. Their leader was Hernando Robinson, a twelve-year-old whom Oliver Twist would have understood immediately. As Hernando and his gang chatted about glue-sniffing and robbery and squabbled over my cheese sandwiches, I tried to referee and to keep down my feelings of guilt over the easy comfort of the world I came from. There is an awkward fact which tends to surface in my mind at such moments, and it came back to me then, surrounded by hungry kids. The fact is that enough grain is produced by the United States alone to eliminate hunger from the planet — if it were to be distributed. But such a thing is unimaginable of course, and the best that Colombia manages for its hungry young *gamines* is to support a charity which has made remarkable progress in bringing them back into society. The government even prints special bank notes for use only in that charity's 'Republic of the Boys' where the *gamines* are turned slowly into citizens. But of course the charity is small and Colombia's orphans of the dark streets are many.

But it was their big brothers who presented Colombia's most serious crime problem. Colombia had a mafia so rich and so powerful that it threatened to corrupt the state. One ex-*gamine* who had risen through the mafia ranks from drug-runner to hit-man to multi-millionaire had managed to get himself elected to Congress. Another mafia boss was even proposing to run for the Presidency. The mafia's sense of their own importance had become such that when BB ordered an assault on their secret cocaine factories, they felt not so much threatened as outraged and they vented their indignation by murdering the President's close friend, the Justice Minister.

So many dollars had come into the mafia's hands from their cocaine exports to the USA that the Colombian economy was threatened with distortion. Colombia's top mafiosi were ranked among the richest men in the world. And because these men could offer vast bribes, a demoralising belief was growing in Colombia that there was almost no official whom the mafia would not be able to buy. Every man has his price, people said. The threat was and is formidable. So far Betancur's response has been to do both the obvious and also the unexpected. He has done the obvious in ordering army assaults on mafia drug routes and cocaine factories, and in showing that corruption was unacceptable whether it stemmed from the mafia or even from the most reputable citizens. A well-known banking family, whose fraudulent operations had gone unchecked for years until the arrival of BB, found their business briskly closed down and one of their leading members reduced from an

(Above right)
A party for rich children.

(Below right) *Tomorrow's lunch — armadillo.*

(Above) Colombia's Carribean coast . . .

(Left) . . . and its Mafia zoo . . .

(Right) . . . and one of its rising generation, living on the town tip.

apparent pillar of society to a convict; to help combat the risk of bribery of officials, BB set an example by opening his own accounts to public inspection on taking office and promising to do it again when his term finished; to encourage a spirit of public service, the President joined queues waiting to be served by bureaucrats and doctors who had over-stayed their lunch hours and, when the shocked public servants arrived, he presented them with an ultimatum: 'Either serve the people or quit your privileged jobs and join them'. And then, trying a more unorthodox approach, the President had decided that since Colombia was full of mafia dollars, he would try to make them work for the nation rather than being kept underground. He offered mafia millionaires a chance to buy respectability. If they put large parts of their fortunes into public works no questions would be asked about how the money had been made. The mafia response had so far included a major slum clearance scheme financed entirely by one mafioso — a man described as a genius of crime had been transformed into a public benefactor.

But, like all of the enduring problems of South America which Belisario Betancur was confronting, corruption would not easily be defeated. As we drove across the Andes towards the capital where we would make our departure from South America, we stopped at a zoo. It was large, quite well stocked, open free to the public, and it was the play-thing of a well-known mafia boss. Because this Godfather had imported the animals illegally, public officials had intervened and confiscated them all. But, mysteriously, the officials had then auctioned the animals, and the man who had bought every last giraffe and elephant and rhino — at giveaway prices and utterly unopposed by any rival bidder — had been the mafia boss. However much you admired the President's attempt to change his country, once you were standing among those mafia giraffes and elephants, you had to acknowledge that he still had a very long way to go.

As we drove on across Belisario's land towards Bogota and our farewell to South America, I was running through the memories of nearly a year and a half of travelling. Through my mind ran faces, tastes, views, smells, sounds, words, names — the bitter-sweet impressions of a poignant land.

There was the great gulf between rich and poor, with the great houses of the 'haves' in every city and the scrawny poverty of the 'have-nots'; there were the rich children with their nannies and their hired clown at a party in one Colombian town and the poor children a few miles away, scavenging in the steaming filth of the town tip... There was the insight into South American macho given me by two off-duty pilots. They'd sat behind me on an internal flight, discussing the style of the man who was handling our destiny up in front. They had tutted and groaned at his hedge-hopping approach to a mountain runway, at his dare-devil landing, and then at his reckless yanking of the big jet into the first runway exit so fast that we were thrown sideways in our seats. 'Awful', said one of the pilots behind me, 'and so typical of us Latins. No *gringo* pilot — no American or European — would ever dream of taking risks like that...'

There was the casual cruelty I'd seen too often in South America: a girl smiling as a armadillo cringed and the machete fell; a live butterfly on a thread; a beatle on a lead; a horse with its jaw roped tight against its chest; a parrot stuffed into a pouch; the shining eyes of men at a cockfight...

There was the struggle of poor governments to keep up appearances. One consulate had been housed in such a small building that visas could only be handed out through a side window to us in the waiting room — the garden.

And, as the van drew nearer to the airport where we would depart from the continent, I checked my wallet and remembered the thefts we had suffered, the need to hide your cash in your sock, the hurrying through dangerous streets at night. 'When things get rough' one local had said, 'this street's like a butcher's shop...'

But far more than the violence, the cruelty and the poverty, I was remembering the warmth and the vitality. Above all, that was what coloured life for me among the South Americans: their determination to look you in the eye and communicate with you, so that just buying an ice cream became an encounter with another soul. 'I live in South America', one Australian had said, 'because it's so alive that at the end of each day I feel I've really lived that day'.

I remembered a little girl in a village where we filmed, watching us and then coming over. At ten years old this South American was a lady with a fine relish for life. She had decided we were the most interesting thing in town at that moment so naturally she would cultivate us. Naturally a South American would go without hesitation towards whatever was interesting; that impulse overcame her childish shyness, and gave her the power to bring us close to her. She did it with bright eyes and laughter, crossing barriers of language, race and age as if they didn't exist. She **was** South America, so for her they really didn't exist. And later, when I climbed into the crew van to drive away, she came to my window. She wanted to make sure she had me. With wide eyes the child asked me for my name: 'Jack'. She took possession of it, and I watched her thoughtfully storing it away in some place inside her where she kept warm memories. Two souls had touched. She had made them touch — that was what life was for. She said, 'And I am Gabriela'. She smiled, South America smiled, and the van drove away.

Wait for me, please, Gabriela! I've a feeling I'll be coming back.

Cartagena
Palenque
CARACAS
VENEZUELA
La Loma
Medellin
BOGOTA
COLOMBIA
THE GUYANAS
N
QUITO
Otavalo
Belem
ECUADOR
Manaus
Iquitos
THE AMAZON
Carajas
Puca llpa
PERU
BRAZIL
LIMA
Machu Picchu
Salvador
Cuzco
Ollantaytambo
(Bahia)
BOLIVIA
Lake Titicaca
BRASILIA
LA PAZ
Oruro
Cochabamba
Potosi
Iquique
PARAGUAY
PACIFIC OCEAN
São Paulo
Rio de Janeiro
ASUNCION
ATLANTIC OCEAN
Ita Caabo
CHILE
URUGUAY
Valparaiso
SANTIAGO
Lujan
MONTEVIDEO
BUENOS AIRES
ARGENTINA

SOUTH
AMERICA

● CAPITAL CITY
• TOWN
○ SITE MENTIONED IN TEXT
▨ JUNGLE
▨ ANDES

ACKNOWLEDGMENTS

THANKS to literally hundreds of South Americans who gave their help and gave it with what the novelist W H Hudson called a century ago 'the innate courtesy and native grace of the Spanish American'. Among them were Gustavo Garcia, Padre Jorge Henriquez, Roman Medina, Fernando Barrero, Irma Siegert de Garcia, Pepe Torres, Nelly and Miguel Sussini, Nina de Friedman, Luis Eduardo Borgeth, John and Betty Adams, Baroness Lida Von Schey, Alec Bright and Maria Eugenia de Ospina...

To the production team, without whom there'd be no film series, no photographs, no book: Producers Geoffrey Barnes and Clive Fleury; Cameraman Pieter de Vries; Camera Assistant Marc Spicer; Sound Recordist Scott Hartford Davis; Film Editors Robin Archer, Paul Cantwell, Chris Spurr and Peter Vile and their assistants Annette Davey, Meredith Hopes, Peter Rothwell and Craig Wood; Researchers Gloria Siegert and Sarita Kendall, plus other researchers and consultants who joined them on location — Lucia Viana, Tim Ross, Paulina Fermandois, Warren Duncan, Maria Cristina Acha, Elizabeth Herrington, Chris Picard and Mariana Novoa...

To the series Executive Producer Peter Reid, the pre-production executive Andrew Lloyd James, the Production Manager John Wilkinson; and to our consultants Dr Miguel Bretos and Dr Jim Levy of the University of NSW, and Professor J C Robinson of California State University and his fellow Latinists who advised us...

And to the Australian Broadcasting Corporation for tackling the whole dauntingly expensive enterprise and seeing it through.

PHOTO CREDITS

HORIZON/James Latter Front cover

Pieter de Vries Pages 10 (below), 17, 25 (above), 39, 41, 50, 59 (below left), 66-67, 70 (below left), 81, 84, 86 (above), 87 (above), 91 (above), 114 (above, below left), 125, 140, 144-145, 151, 154, 158, 160 (above), 172 (above, below), 173 (below), 187.

Warren Duncan Pages 11, 12, 13, 18, 36, 37, 78-79, 83 (centre, above right), 86 (below), 87 (below), 90, 91 (below), 94 (above, centre and below right), 122, 126 (above, below), 127, 129, 133 (above), 145 (above, below), 148, 149, 152 (below), 153, 156 (above left, above right and below), 157, 161, 192.

Scott Hartford-Davis Pages 14, 25 (below), 65, 66 (below), 70 (below right), 71 (above, below), 83 (below), 98, 102, 103, 104, 106 (below right), 110 (above, below), 136 (above, below), 168 (below).

Gloria Siegert Pages 6, 10 (above), 15 (above, below), 29, 32, 36 (above left, below), 40, 41 (below left and right), 44, 45 (above right, below left), 48 (above), 51, 58 (below), 59 (above, below right), 63, 66 (above), 70 (above left and right), 73, 74, 82, 83 (above), 89, 94 (below right), 97, 106 (below left), 108, 111 (above right, centre left), 114 (centre), 114-115, 116 (above, below), 118, 131, 132, 133 (below), 137, 138, 146, 147, 152 (above), 160 (below), 162, 164, 167, 169 (above right), 170, 173 (above), 176, 185 (above), 186 (below), back cover.

Marc Spicer Pages 20-21, 24 (above, below), 28, 45 (below right), 48, 54, 58 (above), 62, 106 (above), 111 (above left), 123, 169 (below), 175, 178-179, 180, 182 (above, below), 183 (above, below), 185 (below), 186 (above).